GREEK HISTORICAL INSCRIPTIONS

359 – 323 B.C.

translated with Introduction and Commentaries by

P. J. RHODES

PREFACE

The history of Greece and Rome is increasingly studied by people with little or no knowledge of the Greek and Latin languages. The major literary sources are readily available in translation, but until recently inscriptions have been accessible only to those who could read the original texts, and the student who could not read the texts has been cut off from an important part of the evidence for the history he has been studying. This set of translations was originally made for the use of a General Degree class in the University of Durham, and is now published, with an introduction and commentaries, in the hope that it will be useful in other universities, and in the sixth forms of schools.

All but one of the texts translated here will be found in the second volume of M. N. Tod's Selection of Greek Historical Inscriptions; with a very few exceptions I have translated the texts as he printed them, and my translations and commentaries owe a great deal to his notes: I am very grateful to the Delegates of the Clarendon Press for permission to make use of his work in this way. I should also like to thank the LACT Ancient History Group, for agreeing to add to its LACTOR series a volume not at present required by the JACT Advanced Level syllabuses, Dr. D. M. Lewis, who read my penultimate draft, and the pupils for whom I first translated these texts.

Durham,

Long Vacation, 1971.

P. J. R.

In this new edition I have corrected some small errors and have modified the notes on nos. 17, 18, 19 and 23.

Michaelmas Term, 1986.

P. J. R.

INTRODUCTION

I

Nowadays inscriptions on stone are used in two main contexts: on public buildings (to announce the identity of the building, or to record the laying of the foundation stone) and on tombstones. In the ancient world, with no wireless or television, and no form of printing, inscribed stones were used not only for these purposes but for many others as well. Public announcements could not be made in the newspapers or delivered to individual members of the public: either a proclamation had to be made at a meeting attended by large numbers of the citizens, or a text would be set up in the centre of the city in the hope that members of the public would come and read it. Temporary notices — lists of candidates for office, proposals for new legislation, and the like — were written on whitewashed boards, and have not survived for us to read; for permanent publication bronze or wood were sometimes used, but the normal medium was stone. Texts of a city's laws and decrees, and of its alliances with other cities; schedules of work on a public building project, and accounts of public expenditure on the project; epigrams commemorating a famous victory, honours voted to a native or foreign benefactor, lists of magistrates, priests and councillors — all these might be inscribed on stone for the citizens to read.

Very large blocks of stone were sometimes used for extensive documents or series of documents (in this collection, no.1 measures about 6' 4" x 1' 6" x 5½", no.9 measures about 7' 1" x 1' 10" x 6¼"), but Greek inscriptions were not necessarily "monumental". Very often the stele would be a slab of stone no larger than an English tombstone (no.11 measures 1' 8" x 1' x 2¼", no.14 1' 9" x 1' 5" x 3¼", no.16 3' 9" x 10½" x 2¾"), and on these and the larger stelae the text was inscribed in letters about a quarter of an inch high. Documents emanating from the public authorities were normally published at public expense; but sometimes a man who had been honoured would himself pay for the publication of his honours. (Publication was not cheap. In Athens it was common in this period to specify in advance how much the state would spend on the stele: no.1, a large stone, and earlier than the others in this collection, cost 60 drachmae; 30 drachmae were allowed for the even larger no.9, and for the elaborate no.10 (but see commentary), and also for the small no.14; surprisingly, only 20 drachmae were allowed for two copies of no.15, though the stone containing our surviving copy measures about 5' 2" x 1' 5" x 4¼" and has at the top a sculptured relief). The stele would be set up in a public place, commonly on the acropolis (the rocky citadel) or in the agora (the main square) of the city. Sometimes more than one copy of a text would be published — an alliance, naturally, would be published in each of the cities participating; no.4 was published in three places within Athens, and no.15 in two places — and where more than one copy of a text has been found it has become apparent that the Greeks lacked our notion of word-for-word accuracy: instead they seem to have held the potentially dangerous belief that, as long as the sense was correctly recorded, the exact wording did not matter.

Some stelae have survived intact — unbroken and completely legible. Far more often, however, only part of the original text survives, and modern scholars have done their best to reconstruct the full text. Where only a few letters on the edges of the stele are missing, restoration is easy, often inevitable; where large parts of the text are missing, reconstruction is far more difficult. If the historical context to which a document belongs can be identified, this may provide clues as to what the missing parts of the text should have contained; if a piece of standardised documentary language can be recognised, this can be reconstructed by comparison with other documents (though small variations are found even within "standard" formulaic expressions). When two or three lines have been correctly restored, the approximate length of the lines is fixed, and this limits the possibilities of restoration in the rest of the document. (Most Athenian decrees of this period were inscribed in a style known as stoichedon, with the letters regularly spaced on a grid, precisely the same number of letters in each line, no spaces between words, and little or no punctuation. This cannot have made for easy reading at the time; but for us it has the advantage that very often a formulaic expression can be found which allows enough reconstruction at one point to reveal the exact number of letters to be restored in each line.) Of the texts in this collection there are few where there is no doubt about any word; but I have included none where the general meaning is not clear.

II

Most of the documents in this collection are Athenian, and some information on the mechanics of the fourth-century Athenian constitution will help to make them intelligible.

The citizens of Athens had been organised since the reforms of Cleisthenes (508/7) in ten tribes:—

I	Erechtheis	VI	Oeneis
II	Aegeis	VII	Cecropis
III	Pandionis	VIII	Hippothontis
IV	Leontis	IX	Aiantis
V	Acamantis	X	Antiochis

The tribes in turn were made up of 139 demes (small local units). To be a citizen of Athens a man had to belong to a deme and the tribe of which that deme formed a part (membership of these units was hereditary: by the fourth century not all Athenians lived in the demes in which they were registered); and a good deal of Athens' governmental machinery was based on this structure.

The sovereign body was an assembly (ecclesia) of all citizens; but there are limits to what can be done by a large body, meeting infrequently (there were 40 regular meetings a year; 6,000 is found as a quorum figure for some categories of business), and day-to-day affairs were in the hands of the council (boule) of five hundred. This body comprised 50 members from each tribe; within the tribe seats were allocated to demes in proportion to their size. Appointment was made by lot from those who stood as candidates; service was for one year at a time, and no man could serve for more than two years in his life. Within the council, the 50 members from each tribe in turn served as the standing committee (prytany) for a tenth of the year (in an order fixed by lot): all business went to them in the first instance; each day one of their members was chosen, again by lot, to be chairman (epistates), and for 24 hours he and some of his colleagues were permanently on duty. In the fifth century one of the duties of the prytany and its chairman had been to preside at meetings of the council and assembly. By the early 370's they had been relieved of this duty, and meetings were instead presided over by a board of proedri — nine members of the council (one from each tribe except the tribe in prytany), one of them designated as epistates, chosen by lot for one day.

Two methods of legislation were available in fourth-century Athens, the one more commonly used being by decree of the assembly. Every matter on which the assembly was to make up its mind was first discussed by the council, which drew up the assembly's agenda (if a topic was given its first airing in the assembly it would then be referred to the council, with instructions to bring the matter back to a later assembly: e.g. no.4). On each matter which it sent forward to the assembly, the council issued its own resolution, the probouleuma. Sometimes the probouleuma contained a positive recommendation, which the assembly might, if it chose, accept as it stood (e.g. no.7, which contains the "probouleumatic formula": "The proedri to whose lot it falls to preside in the next assembly shall bring before the people . . . and put to the people the opinion of the council, that it seems good to the council to accept the alliance"); on other occasions the council put a question to the assembly without making any recommendation of its own (as in no.16: first we have the probouleuma — "it seems good to the council that . . . the people . . . should decide as it thinks best" — and then follows the resultant decree of the assembly); sometimes the council made its own suggestions up to a certain point but left some details open. The probouleuma was read out at the beginning of the debate in the assembly; then — whether or not it had contained a positive recommendation — members were free to propose alternative motions, to propose amendments to a motion already before the assembly (if an amendment was carried, it was published after the original motion which it modified: e.g. nos.9, 10), or to amend a motion by taking it over and re-writing it (this can be detected only in the rare cases where the original motion has been published with the final version: no example here). When the assembly approved a recommendation of the council, the council's "probouleumatic formula" was often left in the published version of the text.

The alternative to a decree of the assembly was a law (nomos). At the end of the fifth century, the accumulation of nearly two hundred years' decrees had produced a great deal of confusion, and an attempt was then made to assemble all currently valid measures in an organised code of laws. Thereafter, in theory, matters of general and permanent application were to be dealt with by laws; decrees were to be reserved for subsidiary and temporary enactments, and were to rank below laws in importance and validity. How the new law-making procedure (nomothesia) worked is not certain: the final decision lay not with the council and assembly but with a special board of nomothetae; references in speeches of the fourth century suggest that the procedure should have resembled that of a law-court, with the nomothetae sitting in judgment on the existing law code and the new proposal; but the surviving texts of laws (the only one in this collection is no.15) have introductory material which matches that of decrees as closely as possible. In practice, this new procedure seems to have been used very little: it was more cumbersome than the procedure for making decrees, and the Athenians continued for the most part to legislate by decree (one matter for which they did use the new procedure was the annual budget, on which see below), and to accumulate a new set of uncertainties and contradictions. When the proposer of a new measure did put forward a law rather than a decree, his object was probably to confer extra importance and solemnity on his enactment.

By the fourth century the layout of an Athenian law or decree had become more or less standardised. Not every text contained every possible element, but in a complete text we should find the following:—

1.   The stele was often surmounted by a pediment, and sometimes contained a sculptured relief above and/or below the text. (No.10 has reliefs above and below the text; no.15 has a pediment and relief above).

2. Heading, in larger letters (for easy identification of text):
   invocation: "Gods" (perhaps reflecting the prayer with which proceedings in the
       assembly began)   (nos. 10, 16)
   archon and/or secretary of the year   (nos. 1, 7, 9)
   subject of decree   (nos. 9, 10, 21)

3. Prescript (details of date, &c., from the secretary's records):
   archon of the year (since we know the names of all the archons from 480 to the end of
       the fourth century, this provides us with the most reliable means of dating a decree)
   prytany: the name of the tribe, and its number in that year's sequence of prytanies
   secretary of the year
   date in calendar, and day within prytany
   chairman of the day, who "put the question"
   enactment-formula: either (a) "resolved by the people", or (b) "resolved by the council
       and people", or (c) "resolved by the nomothetae". (In decrees, b was normal when
       the assembly adopted a proposal of the council, a in other cases, but sometimes the
       wrong formula was used; c was used in laws.)
                                   (The prescripts of nos. 14 and 21 contain all these elements.)

4. The main text of the decree or law:
   often beginning: "for the good fortune of the people of Athens"   (nos. 1, 7, 15, 22)
   reason for enactment
   motion-formula: either (a) "the people shall resolve" (when the motion is not a recom-
       mendation of the council), or (b) the probouleumatic formula (when the assembly
       adopts a recommendation of the council: compare p. v, above), or (c) "the
       nomothetae shall resolve"
   and then the positive proposals, commonly ending with entertainment at dinner in the
       town hall (prytaneum) for envoys or the recipients of honours   (nos. 3, 7, 9, 10, 11)
   orders for the publication of the text   (nos. 1, 3, 4, 9, 10, 14, 15, 21)

5. Amendments:
   were published after the original motion. They normally begin with:
   proposer of amendment   (omitted in no. 10)
   either (a) "in other respects in accordance with [the proposer of the original motion]"
       (when the original motion was not a recommendation of the council), or (b) "in
       other respects in accordance with the council"   (nos. 9, 10)

Athenian administration was based on the principle that any good citizen could and should play a modest part in the running of the state: large numbers of annual boards were set up (mostly of ten men, one picked by lot from the candidates in each tribe), and were given strictly limited jobs to do; all worked under the general supervision of the council, which also had judicial powers in matters concerning the running of the state. From the middle of the fourth century there was a move away from this interpretation of democracy towards entrusting greater powers to men of proved ability, but in matters illustrated by the texts in this collection there was little change.

The collection of taxes was not made by state officials, but was farmed out to contractors. The contract (like other state contracts, e.g. for rentals or public works) was auctioned to the highest bidder, in the presence of the council, by the sellers (poletae); in due course the contractor had to pay the sum agreed (irrespective of the amount he had actually

ollected) to the receivers (apodectae), again in the presence of the council; if he defaulted
e would be pursued by a board of exacters (practores). In the fifth century all revenue was
aid into a central treasury, and all state payments were made from that treasury — by yet
nother board. In the fourth century the apodectae made an allocation (merismos) to various
bending authorities: amongst these authorities were the assembly, which had an expense
ccount, administered by the "treasurer of the people" (I translate the fund's official title
s "the people's fund for expenditure on decrees"), and the council, which had a similar
xpense account. Two other funds, over which there was some controversy between the 350's
nd the 330's, were the theoric fund (established to make grants to cover the cost of theatre
ickets at festivals; but its activities were extended beyond this) and the military (stratiotic)
und. The year's allocations to spending authorities were fixed by a law and could only be
ltered by a law: in no. 9 (a decree) the cost of crowns for the sons of Leucon is accepted
or future years as a charge on the assembly's expense account (which will have to be given
n increased allocation for the purpose); but in the year when the decree was carried the fund
lid not have enough money for these crowns, so for that year the apodectae were ordered to
ake the cost of the crowns from the money which they would otherwise allocate to the
tratiotic fund.

One area in which the fourth century saw an increase in professionalism was the office
of secretary. Until the 360's the principal state secretary, who kept the records of the council
ind assembly, and was responsible for publishing documents when required, was a member
of the council, serving for one prytany (a tenth of a year) only. In the 360's there was a
change: the office was detached from membership of the council, and service was now for a
year. Curiously, it is almost certain that after this change two different titles — "secretary to
the council" and "secretary by the prytany" — were used indiscriminately to denote the
same official.

Each Greek city had its own calendar. Years were not counted from any real or imagined
fixed point (the Olympic records, counting from a first festival in 776 B.C., could be used to
correlate the systems of different cities; but their four-yearly basis was inconvenient, and so
this system did not pass into everyday use), but were identified by reference to an eponymous
magistrate, who gave his name to the year in which he served. In Athens the eponymous
magistrate was the archon: thus the year which we call 378/7 (summer 378 — summer 377:
the year in which no.1 was enacted) was to the Athenians the year of Nausinicus' archonship.
In Athens, as in most cities, the year was not a solar year of c.365 days, but was based on
lunar months, of 29 or 30 days. In an "ordinary" year of 12 months, there were c.354 days;
in an "intercalary" year a thirteenth month was added and there were c.384 days. Decisions
as to how long particular months were to be, and how many months there were to be in a
particular year (in Athens, as in many but not all cities, the year was probably supposed to
begin at the first new moon after the summer solstice) seem to have been taken on an ad hoc
basis, not in accordance with a regular rule; and what was decided one way in Athens might
be decided differently elsewhere. Because of these irregularities it is rarely possible to give
the exact equivalents in our calendar of dates in a Greek calendar. The names of the months
at Athens were:—

i	Hecatombaeon	vii	Gamelion
ii	Metageitnion	viii	Anthesterion
iii	Boedromion	ix	Elaphebolion
iv	Pyanopsion	x	Munychion
v	Maemacterion	xi	Thargelion
vi	Posideon	xii	Scirophorion

Hecatombaeon corresponded roughly to our July, and so on. In intercalary years the extra month was usually a second Posideon, added after the first.

The same names were used in different cities for units of money, but the values of the different currencies varied in accordance with the weights of silver to which the names were applied in each city. The scale used in Athens was:—

6 obols	=	1 drachma
100 drachmae	=	1 mina
60 minas	=	1 talent

(Sums of money were often expressed in talents, drachmae and obols, without the use of the mina as an intermediate unit. For the "stater" as a standard coin, see the commentary on nos. 8 and 17.) In the second half of the fourth century payments for attending meetings of public bodies (juries, the council, the assembly, &c.) varied between ½ and 1½ drachmae a day; an unskilled labourer could earn 1½ drachmae a day, a skilled 2 or 2½ drachmae; a man was regarded as rich enough to be liable to such burdens as the trierarchy (cf. commentary on no. 22) if his total property was worth about 4 talents, and would have been one of the richest Athenian citizens if his property was worth as much as 15 talents; in 341 Demosthenes claimed that in the past few years the annual revenue of Athens had increased from 130 talents to 400 talents.

III

The texts in this collection are arranged in chronological order. The Greek texts have been edited and published in various places: I give before the translation those references which the English sixth-former or undergraduate is most likely to meet in his reading; with a few exceptions, which I note, the text which I translate is that of the edition which I name last.

In editions of the original texts, letters which are not visible on the stone but have been restored by editors (sometimes with certainty, sometimes very uncertainly) are enclosed in square brackets. This does not seem feasible in a collection of translations: instead I begin the commentary on each inscription with a note on how far the Greek text is preserved. I have used pointed brackets — ⟨ ⟩ — in the translations to enclose words which are not present in the Greek text but have been added by way of explanation (one or two expansions of standard expressions have been made at their first appearance only). The division of the texts into paragraphs is my own: for ease of reference I give in the left-hand margin the number of the line in the Greek text which corresponds to the beginning of each of my paragraphs. Parts of the translations which are printed in block capitals correspond to sections of the Greek text inscribed in larger letters.

Transliteration of Greek words and names has been a matter of controversy for a long time. Most scholars have found themselves driven to use an awkward compromise between Latin and Latin-like forms and direct, letter-for-letter transliteration: I have unashamedly leaned further in the direction of Latin than is fashionable.

In the commentaries I have tried to give enough background information for the documents to be appreciated in their historical context, and to explain technicalities in the texts; but technicalities which have been explained in this Introduction are not explained again.

ABBREVIATIONS

Hesp.   Hesperia, the journal of the American School of Classical Studies at Athens.
         Published quarterly from 1932.

IG   Inscriptiones Graecae. Berlin: Reimer / De Gruyter, for the German Academy
         of Sciences. I cite the following volumes:
         ii²   second edition of ii, ed. J. Kirchner, 1913—40.
                  (Cited in some books as ii—iii².)
         vii   ed. W. Dittenberger, 1892.
         XII.ii   ed. G. R. Paton, 1899.
         XII.vii ed. J. Delamarre, 1908.

OGIS   W. Dittenberger (ed.), Orientis Graeci Inscriptiones Selectae.
         Leipzig: Hirzel, 1903—5.

SEG   Supplementum Epigraphicum Graecum. Leiden: Sijthoff, published
         intermittently from 1923.

SIG³   W. Dittenberger (ed.), Sylloge Inscriptionum Graecarum. 3rd edition.
         Leipzig: Hirzel, 1915—24.

Tod   M. N. Tod (ed.), A Selection of Greek Historical Inscriptions, volume ii.
         From 403 to 323 B.C. Oxford: Clarendon Press, 1948.

         I also cite (by its title)
F. Hiller von Gaertringen (ed.), Inschriften von Priene. Berlin: Reimer, for the
         Royal Museum, 1906.

Prospectus of the Second Athenian League, 378/7

(IG ii² 43, SIG³ 147, Tod 123)

A. The Main Face of the Stele
1 IN THE ARCHONSHIP OF NAUSINICUS ⟨378/7⟩;
CALLIBIUS, SON OF CEPHISOPHON, OF ⟨THE DEME⟩ PAEANIA,
WAS SECRETARY.

4 In the seventh prytany, of ⟨the tribe⟩ Hippothontis; resolved by the
council and people; Charinus, of ⟨the deme⟩ Athmonum, was chairman;
Aristoteles proposed:—

7 For the good fortune of the Athenians and of the Athenians' allies; so
that the Spartans shall allow the Greeks to be free and independent, and
to live at peace in secure occupation of all their own territory; and so
that the common peace sworn by the Greeks and the ⟨Persian⟩ King in
accordance with the agreed terms may prevail and last for ever; the
people shall resolve:

15 If any of the Greeks or of the barbarians living in Europe or of the
islanders, who are not subject to the ⟨Persian⟩ King, wishes to be an
ally of the Athenians and their allies, he may be — ⟨remaining⟩ free and
independent, being governed under whatever constitution he wishes,
without receiving a garrison or submitting to a governor or paying tribute,
on the same terms as the Chians, the Thebans and the other allies. For
those who make alliance with the Athenians and their allies, the people
shall renounce whatever Athenian possessions whether public or private
there may be in the territory of those who make the alliance, and shall
give them guarantees of this. If there are in Athens stelae unfavourable
to any of the cities which makes alliance with Athens, the council currently in office shall have authority to demolish them.

35 From the archonship of Nausinicus it shall be illegal for any Athenian to
own either publicly or privately, by purchase or by mortgage or in any
other way whatever, any house or land in the territory of the allies. If
any one does buy, acquire or take out a mortgage on ⟨such property⟩
in any way, any of the allies who wishes may report him to the delegates
of the allies: the delegates shall sell ⟨the property⟩ and give half ⟨the

proceeds⟩ to the informer, while the other half shall be the common property of the allies.

46　If any one makes war by land or by sea on those who have made the alliance, the Athenians and the allies shall go to support these by land and by sea with all their forces so far as they are able.

51　If any official or private citizen proposes or ⟨as chairman⟩ puts to the vote a proposal against this decree, that any of the things stated in this decree should be annulled, he may be deprived of his political rights, and his property shall be confiscated, a tenth being dedicated to the goddess ⟨Athena⟩: he shall be tried by the Athenians and the allies for breaking up the alliance, and shall be sentenced to death or to exile from the territory controlled by the Athenians and the allies; if he is condemned to death, he shall not be buried in the territory of the Athenians and the allies.

63　The secretary of the council shall inscribe this decree on a stone stele and erect it beside ⟨the statue of⟩ Zeus Eleutherios; the sum of 60 drachmae for the inscription of the stele shall be provided from the fund of 10 talents by the treasurers of the goddess ⟨Athena⟩. On the stele shall be inscribed the names of the cities which are allies, and of any other which becomes an ally. This is to be inscribed.

72　The people shall choose at once three envoys to Thebes, to persuade the Thebans of what advantages they can. (The following were chosen: Aristoteles of Marathon; Pyrrhander of Anaphlystus; Thrasybulus of Collytus.)

78　The following cities are allies of the Athenians:—

79　(in the same hand as the decree)　　　Chios, Mytilene, Methymna, Rhodes, Byzantium;

(heading a second column — same hand again)　　　Thebes;

(second hand, continuing second column: cities joining before end of 378/7)　　　Chalcis, Eretria, Arethusa, Carystus, Icus;

(third hand, continuing first column: gains of 377)　　　Perinthus, Peparethus, Sciathus, Maronea, Dium (Euboea);

(other names on main face: gains of 376?)	Tenedos, Poeessa, Paros, Athenae Diades, Pall—, (other names, irrecoverable);

B. The Left Hand Side of the Stele

131	(beginning at the same level as the first entries in the list on the main face)	The demos of the Zacynthians in Nellus;
97	(beginning near the level of the top of the decree and continuing to about three quarters of the way down: large gap between the end of this list and the entry noted above. All gains of 375?)	The demos of the Theraeans, Abdera, Thasos, Chalcidians from Thrace, Aenus, Samothrace, Dicaeopolis, Acarnania, Cephallenia, Pronni, Alcetas ⟨of the Molossi⟩ , Neoptolemus ⟨his son⟩ , (an erasure), Andros, Tenos, Hestiaea, Myconus, Antissa, Eresus, Astraeus; from Ceos: Iulis, Coresia, Carthaea; Elaeus, Amorgus, Selymbria, Siphnus, Sicinus, Thracian Dium, Neapolis.

91 Below the list on the main face begins another decree in the name of Aristoteles, too fragmentary to be translated.

Most of the inscribed surface of the stone is preserved, and except where otherwise noted the text is not seriously in doubt. The clause underlined in the paragraph beginning at 7 was later erased, with near-success (at a time when the Athenians no longer wished to be polite to the Persians): the restoration is somewhat conjectural. In the paragraph beginning at 15 "in Europe" is the restoration of H. T. Wade-Gery, noted in Tod's Addenda: the editions cited restore "on the mainland". In the section of the list of names beginning at 97, "Theraeans" is the restoration of J. E. Coleman and D. W. Bradeen (Hesp. xxxvi 1967, 102-4) they point out that there is not enough room on the stone for the restoration of the editions cited, "Corcyraeans". In the erasure later in this section editors have restored "Jason ⟨tyrant of Pherae⟩ ", and have believed that part of the last letter is visible at the end of the erasure; but the erasure seems too long for that mark to belong to a five-letter name.

This inscription is some twenty years earlier than any of the others in this collection, but is included because the league which it advertised remained in existence until 338/7 and in some respects served as a model for the League of Corinth then founded by Philip of Macedon (cf. nos. 13 and 17—19 with commentary). In 386 Sparta and Persia had combined to force on the Greeks a common peace treaty, by which the Greeks of Asia Minor were ceded to Persia, and all other Greek cities (with a few exceptions) were to be free and independent. To Athens the terms were unwelcome, but had to be accepted: when she made an alliance with Chios in 384/3 (alluded to in the paragraph beginning at 15) it was very clearly stated that the alliance was to be within the framework of the common peace; and the same stipulation is made in this document. Sparta hoped to exploit the peace terms to her advantage, and in 382 added to her unpopularity by occupying the city of Thebes. Exiles from Thebes fled to Athens, and in the winter of 379/8 set out from Athens to liberate Thebes. It was at this point that Athenians decided to unite the Chians and other allies with whom they had similar treaties in an anti-Spartan league, to which Thebes was added when tactless behaviour by Sparta in 378 commited Athens firmly to the Theban side. Early in 377, with the league already in being, this prospectus was issued. The paragraphs beginning at 15 and 35 guarantee the independence of the member states, promising, in effect, that this league will not degenerate into an Athenian empire as the anti-Persian Delian League had done in the fifth century. In fact this league did degenerate in the same way as the Delian League, and for the same reason. The Delian League was maintained in existence and exploited to Athens' advantage when it was no longer necessary to fight against Persia; Thebes' defeat of Sparta at Leuctra in 371 made it unnecessary for this league to continue to resist Spartan aggression, and Athens found herself instead combining with Sparta against Thebes, while in the Aegean she revived territorial ambitions in the north which were bound to alarm members of the league. Promises made in this prospectus were broken, in spirit if not in the letter: tribute (phoros) was not collected from the members, but by 373 if not earlier the members were made to pay money under the name of "contributions" (syntaxeis); no Athenian settlements were made on the territory of members listed on this stele, but probably after 375 (certainly after 373) additions to this list ceased, and members who joined later found that they were not immune; in the late 360's Athens interfered in the internal affairs of Ceos; and in the 350's — before and during the Social War of 356—355 — Athens sent governors and garrisons to some member states to secure their loyalty: cf. nos. 5 and 6.

Technically the league was a defensive alliance (cf. paragraph beginning at 46). The member states sent delegates (cf. paragraph beginning at 35) to a synedrion in permanent session in Athens, in which each of the allied states (and perhaps Athens too) had one vote. Matters affecting the allies were first considered by the synedrion and the Athenian council, and the Athenian assembly then took the final decision — but presumably could not commit the allies against the will of the synedrion.

In the paragraph beginning at 63, the fund of 10 talents administered by the treasurers of Athena is one of many devices tried in the first quarter of the fourth century to provide for expenses incurred by the assembly. The assembly's expense account (cf. Introduction, p. vii) was probably set up in 376. There have been various guesses about the object of the embassy to Thebes mentioned in the paragraph beginning at 72: perhaps the Thebans claimed to represent the whole of Boeotia and wanted to join the league as "Boeotians", and the Athenians were trying to dissuade them from this.

2

Alliance between Athens and Thacian Kings, 357

(IG ii² 126, Tod 151)

1   . . . assist . . . and the allies . . . unless it is decided . . . Concerning the
      cities which have been recorded on the stelae as paying tribute to Berisades,

Amadocus or Cersobleptes and as allies of the Athenians: If they do not pay to the Athenians the whole of their syntaxis, Berisades, Amadocus and Cersobleptes shall exact it as far as they are able; and if anywhere they fail to pay to Berisades, Amadocus or Cersobleptes the whole of their tribute, the Athenians and the generals in charge of their force shall exact it as far as they are able. The Greek cities in the Chersonese, paying the traditional tribute to Berisades, Amadocus and Cersobleptes and the syntaxis to the Athenians, shall be free and independent, being allies of the Athenians as they have sworn and also of Berisades, Amadocus and Cersobleptes. If any of the cities secedes from the Athenians, Berisades, Amadocus and Cersobleptes shall render assistance as called on by the Athenians. And if . . .

The beginning and end of the document are lost, and where a text is given about half of each line survives (the repetition of the three kings' names guarantees the length of the lines). I translate Tod's text as modified by B. D. Meritt and others, The Athenian Tribute Lists, II (1949), p. 104, T 78d.

About the end of 360 King Cotys of Thrace was murdered, and the claims of his son Cersobleptes were challenged by two rivals, Berisades and Amadocus. The kingdom included the European shore of the Hellespont and Propontis, and the Athenians, who were always concerned to ensure the safety of their corn supplies from the Black Sea (for which cf. no. 9), and who in the 360's had begun to revive their territorial ambitions in the northern Aegean (cf. commentary on no.1), were anxious to come to a satisfactory arrangement with the rival princes. A series of agreements was attempted, and gave Athens no satisfaction: this inscription presumably represents the final treaty, negotiated by Chares at the end of 357 (cf. commentary on no. 3), by which the three claimants were recognised as joint rulers for some purposes but in general the kingdom was divided between Berisades in the west, Amadocus in the centre and Cersobleptes in the east, and some cities were recognised as being in both the Athenian and the Thracian sphere of influence. For Athens' further dealings with the western kingdom see no. 7; Cersobleptes, in the east, remained independent of Macedon longest, ceding the cities of the Chersonese to Athens in 353/2, being reduced by Philip to the status of vassal king in 346 and finally deposed in 342 (for the sequel, cf. commentary on no. 11).

For the syntaxis paid by members of her league to Athens, see the commentary on no.1: assessment (no.12, paragraph beginning at 22) and expenditure (no. 6, paragraph beginning at 7) of this were apparently the responsibility of the league's synedrion, so (if the text is correctly restored) Athens in making this arrangement was probably exceeding her rights, and the author of this decree, in speaking of the cities' paying their syntaxis "to the Athenians" was certainly disloyal to the spirit in which the league was founded.

Alliance of Athens and Euboean Cities, 357/6

(IG ii² 124, SIG³ 190, Tod 153)

1   ... The secretary by the prytany shall record this decree on the <u>acropolis</u>: the money for the <u>stele</u> shall be provided by the treasurer from the fund for expenditure on decrees.

4   Five men shall be chosen to go and receive the oaths from the Carystians; the oaths shall be sworn to the Carystians by the taxiarchs, the generals and the council ⟨of Athens⟩.

7   Praise the people of the Carystians and their envoys and their delegate ⟨to the <u>synedrion</u> of the league⟩, and invite them to hospitality in the <u>prytaneum</u> tomorrow. Praise also Meno the general and the envoys sent ⟨by Athens⟩ to Carystus, and invite them to dinner in the <u>prytaneum</u> tomorrow: the treasurer of the people shall give them for travelling expenses 20 drachmae from the people's fund for expenditure on decrees. The treasurer of the people shall also give the envoys sent on the missions to Eretria, Chalcis and Hestiaea 20 drachmae each; and the treasurer of the people shall give those who negotiated the alliance 10 drachmae each.

18   The following ⟨Athenians⟩ took the oath:—
The council for the year of Agathocles' archonship ⟨357/6⟩;
These generals:
      Chabrias of Aexone (<u>erased but still legible</u>);
      Cha—;
      Iphicrates of Rhamnus;
      Meno of Potamus;
      Philochares of Rhamnus;
      Execestides of Thoricus;
      Alcimachus of Anagyrus;
      Diocles of Alopece.

The first two paragraphs are largely restored (if the first paragraph is correctly restored, its language is unusually condensed); in the third paragraph there are no gaps of more than a few letters and the text is certain. Much trouble is caused by the list of generals: Chabrias' name has been erased but is still legible; editors have supposed that this was done because he was deposed for mishandling negotiations with the Thracian princes (cf. commentary on no. 2) and so, contrary to expectations, did not swear; and for the second name Chares of

Angele has been restored; but the alternative suggestion has been made that Chares, who negotiated the final settlement with the Thracians late in 357, did not swear to the Euboean alliance (which would ease the chronology of this period — and there must in any case have been two other generals who did not swear to this alliance), and that Chabrias' name was inscribed twice in error and therefore deleted once. (The list of oath-takers does not include the taxiarchs.)

The Euboean cities joined the Second Athenian League, but after Thebes' victory over Sparta in 371 they adhered to Thebes rather than Athens. Probably in 357, conflict between pro-Theban and pro-Athenian parties gave Athens the opportunity to intervene, and she was able to bring the cities back into her league. There was further trouble in Euboea in the 340's when the cities wavered between Athens and Philip of Macedon.

The generals were ten in number, elected annually and capable of being re-elected (at this date they were probably elected as in the later fifth century: one irrespective of tribe, and the other nine representing nine of the ten tribes — the 7 [or 8] listed here belong to 6 [or 7] different tribes): they were the commanders of the Athenian forces; from about the middle of the fourth century there was an increasing tendency to designate certain regular jobs (e.g. the defence of Attica) and allocate them to particular generals for the year: for an example see no. 22, paragraph beginning at 204, with commentary. The taxiarchs were ten in number, one elected annually from each tribe, and commanded their tribal divisions in the Athenian army as subordinates of the general or generals who held the chief command. For the synedrion of the league, see the commentary on no.1. It is interesting to notice that the Athenians regularly invited foreigners to "hospitality" but their own citizens to "dinner". Of the generals mentioned here, Chabrias and Iphicrates had commanded armies for Athens (and, when Athens did not require their services, for other states) since c.390. The Social War ended the careers of both: Chabrias was killed in the battle of Chios (356); Iphicrates was disgraced after refusing battle at Embata (355). Chares first served as a general in the early 360's; fought at Embata when his colleagues refused; and his career continued until the reign of Alexander: for his activities in 340 cf. no.11.

The chronology of the early 350's is uncertain. I believe that Athens' recovery of Euboea occurred in the latter half of 357; the renewed alliances with the Euboean cities were negotiated in the winter of 357/6; Chares negotiated the final settlement with the Thracians (cf. no. 2) about the same time; the Social War (cf. no. 6) filled the summers of 356 and 355. Others have placed the recovery of Euboea early in 357 and the opening campaign of the Social War shortly after it (still in the year 358/7): this inscription is then dated to the autumn of 357, and it is supposed that Chares was the second general on the list and that Chabrias was prevented from swearing by his death in the battle of Chios.

4

Athens aids Eretria, 357 (?)

(IG ii² 125, SIG³ 191, Tod 154)

1   Resolved by the people; Hegesippus proposed:—

1   So that in future none of the allies of the Athenian people, nor any one else, whether foreigner or citizen, shall harm any of the allies, setting out

from Attica or from any of the allied cities; the people shall resolve:

6   Concerning those who have invaded the land of the Eretrians, the council shall make a <u>probouleuma</u> and bring it before the people at the next assembly, so that those men may be punished in accordance with the treaty. And if any one else in future invades Eretria or any of the other allied cities, ⟨whether he be⟩ an Athenian or from the allies of the Athenians, he shall be condemned to death and his property shall be confiscated, a tenth being dedicated to the goddess ⟨Athena⟩: his property shall be recoverable from all the allied cities, and if any city appropriates it, that city shall owe it to the common ⟨fund⟩ of the allies.

17   Record this decree on a stone <u>stele</u>, and erect it on the <u>acropolis</u>, in the <u>agora</u> and in the harbour: the treasurer of the people shall provide the money for the inscription.

20   Praise those who have rendered assistance to Eretria . . . the Carystians . . . the general . . .

Not much more than half of each line survives, but the general sense is clear to line 17; the arrangements for publication are less certain.

No internal evidence guarantees the date of this inscription, but it is best connected with Athens' recovery of Euboea in 357 (cf. no. 3 and commentary: there were further incidents involving the Euboean cities in the 340's, but a declaration guaranteeing members of the league against attack by their fellow-members is perhaps less likely after the league had been weakened by the Social War): it is not known which Athenians or allies had been involved in an attack on Eretria. The measures to be taken against those who attack their fellow-members are comparable to those threatened in the prospectus of the league (no.1, lines 51 sqq.) against any one who attempts to break up the alliance.

Hegesippus, the author of the decree, became prominent as a supporter of Demosthenes in the late 340's; he was also the author of no.14, and his brother Hegesander was the author of no. 6. On the legislative mechanism implied in the paragraph beginning at 6, see the Introduction, p. v: this decree lays down a general rule, and the council is to put the specific questions of the recent attack on Eretria on the agenda of the next assembly.

Arcesine honours Androtion, 356 (?)

(IG XII.vii 5, SIG³ 193, Tod 152)

1   Resolved by the council and people of Arcesine:—

2   Since Androtion has been a good man with regard to the people of
Arcesine, and in governing the city has not caused distress to any of the
citizens or of the foreigners visiting the city; and he lent money to the
city at a critical time and was prepared to forgo the interest; and when
the city was in difficulties he advanced the wages of the garrison himself
and on recovering the money at the end of the year exacted no interest;
and he saved the city twelve minas expenditure each year; and he ran-
somed any men he came across who had been captured by the enemy:

16   Crown Androtion son of Andron, of Athens, with a gold crown of five
hundred drachmae for his virtue, justice and goodwill towards the people
of Arcesine; record him as proxenos and benefactor of the city of
Arcesine, both himself and his descendants; and grant him freedom from
all impositions.

24   Since it has also been resolved by the allies . . . likewise . . .

The stone is intact to line 25, and the text translated is certain.

Arcesine was one of the three cities on the island of Amorgus, which joined the Second
Athenian League in time to be included in the list of members on no.1. Androtion, an Athenian politician and historian, is being honoured for his generous treatment of Arcesine during
a period of at least two years as governor (of Arcesine or of the whole island?): he was a
member of the council in Athens, probably in 356/5, so he perhaps returned to Athens in 356.
The decree shows that Athens has broken one of the promises made in the prospectus of the
league by sending a governor and garrison to Amorgus, not later than 358 (i.e. before the
outbreak of the Social War: cf. commentary on no. 3).

The nearest English word to proxenos is "consul": Androtion and his descendants are
being made hereditary representatives in Athens of the interests of Arcesine. "Freedom from
all impositions" (ateleia) denotes immunity from taxation, military service and all the duties
associated with citizenship of Arcesine.

Andros garrisoned in the Social War, 356

(IG ii² 123, SIG³ 192, Tod 156)

1   In the archonship of Agathocles ⟨357/6⟩; in the ninth prytany, of Aegeis;
when Diodotus son of Diocles, of Angele, was secretary; on the eighth
⟨day⟩ of the prytany. The question was put by Diotimus of Oenoe,
⟨chairman⟩ of the proedri; resolved by the council and people; Hegesander
proposed:—

7   So that Andros may be safe for the people of Athens and the people of
Andros, and so that the garrison on Andros may receive its wages out of
the syntaxeis in accordance with the resolutions of the allies, and the
watch may not be broken off: choose a general out of those who have
been elected, the chosen man to be responsible for Andros. Archedemus
shall exact the monies due from the islands to the soldiers on Andros,
and pass them to the governor on Andros, so that the soldiers may have
their wages . . .

Enough of the inscribed surface survives to make the general sense certain.

Probably in 356 (for chronology cf. the commentary on no. 3), the Social War broke
out, with Rhodes, Chios, Cos and Byzantium attempting to secede from the Second Athenian
League. In 356 the rebels defeated an Athenian force off Chios; they then proceeded to
attack other Aegean islands; in 355 Chares attacked the rebels at Embata (between Chios and
the mainland of Asia Minor), but his colleagues Iphicrates and Timotheus refused to fight
owing to the weather: Chares was defeated, and the rebels succeeded in winning their
independence.

A governor and garrison had been sent to Arcesine before the outbreak of the Social
War (cf. no. 5): the sending of a garrison to Andros was perhaps Athens' reaction to the outbreak of the war, and must have had the consent of the allied synedrion, since this inscription reveals that the allies resolved that the soldiers should be paid from the syntaxeis.
Hegesander was the brother of Hegesippus, the author of nos. 4 and 14.

Athenian Alliance with Thracian, Paeonian and Illyrian Kings, 356

(IG ii² 127, SIG³ 196, Tod 157)

1   SECRETARY LYSIAS SON OF LYS—, OF PITHUS.

2   Alliance of the Athenians with Cetriporis the Thracian and his brothers and with Lyppeius the Paeonian and with Grabus the Illyrian.

4   In the archonship of Elpines ⟨356/5⟩; in the first prytany, of Hippothontis; on the eleventh of the prytany. The question was put by Mnesarchus of — , ⟨chairman⟩ of the proedri; resolved by the council and people; Callisthenes proposed:—

7   For the good fortune of the people of Athens; accept the alliance on the terms which Cetriporis' brother Monunius says his brother agreed with the ⟨representative⟩ sent from the Athenian people to Cetriporis and his brothers and to Lyppeius the Paeonian and to Grabus the Illyrian;

12   And the proedri to whose lot it falls to preside in the next assembly shall bring before the people Cetriporis' brother Monunius, and Pisianax, and the deputations which have come from Lyppeius and Grabus, and —tus who has come from Chares, and put to the people the opinion of the council, that it seems good to the council to accept the alliance, since . . .

19   (lacuna)

26   . . . the money. Praise Cetriporis and his brothers, because they are good men with regard to the people of Athens; praise also Monunius, the brother who has come from Cetriporis, for his virtue and goodwill, and invite him to hospitality in the prytaneum tomorrow. Praise also Pisianax and invite him to dinner in the prytaneum tomorrow. Invite the envoys who have come from the other kings to hospitality in the prytaneum tomorrow.

34   If there is anything lacking in this decree, the council shall have authority ⟨to make supplementary decisions⟩.

36   Chosen as envoys: Lysicrates of Oenoe, Antimachus of —, Thrason of Erchia.

38 I swear by Zeus, by Earth, by Sun, by Poseidon, by Athena and by Ares
    that I shall be a friend and ally to Cetriporis and Cetriporis' brothers,
    and shall wage the war with Cetriporis against Philip without deceit, with
    all my strength, as far as I am able; and I shall not put an end to the war
    against Philip in advance, without ⟨the agreement of⟩ Cetriporis and his
    brothers; and I shall join with Cetriporis and his brothers in overthrowing
    the other places which Philip occupies, and I shall join with Cetriporis
    and his brothers in capturing Crenides; and I shall give back . . .

Three fragments, fairly generously restored.

Philip II succeeded to the throne of Macedon in 359: his claim was challenged by
several rivals, and to keep some enemies content while he dealt with others he dropped
hints of future bargains, but probably avoided making any binding promises.   The
Athenians were led to suppose that if he captured Amphipolis, a city on an important
site near the mouth of the Strymon, which they had colonised in 437/6 but had lost in
the 420's, he would give it to them: in 357 he captured Amphipolis but retained
possession of it himself, and the Athenians in indignation declared war on him.   In 356
Philip was given the opportunity to advance further east, beyond Amphipolis, when the
recently founded Thasian colony of Crenides appealed for help against a Thracian attack;
he occupied the city and refounded it as Philippi.   At this point Athens made the
alliance with various of Philip's barbarian neighbours which is recorded in this inscription: Cetriporis and his brothers were the rulers of the western part of the Thracian
kingdom in succession to their father Berisades, who died in 357/6 (cf. no. 2).   In fact
nothing came of this alliance: Athens was preoccupied with the Social War (cf. commentary on nos. 3 and 6), and in 355 Philip was able to frighten the barbarians into
submission before they were ready to attack him.

On the legislative machinery implied by the paragraphs beginning at 7 and 12, see the
Introduction, p. v. On Chares see the commentary on no. 3. The paragraph beginning
at 34 has its parallels: there were several occasions in the fourth century when the council
was authorised to fill any gaps that might be found in a decree of the assembly (cf. no. 22,
paragraph beginning at 264, and, from Mytilene, no. 23, paragraph beginning at 37). The
envoys in the paragraph beginning at 36 were presumably sent to the barbarian kings to
receive their oaths.

8

Contributions to the Sacred War, c. 355—351

(IG vii 2418, SIG³ 201, Tod 160)

1 The following made contributions to the war which the Boeotians fought
   for the shrine at Delphi against the desecrators of the shrine of Pythian
   Apollo:—

5

In the archonship of Aristion

Alyzea: –. (Envoys: Charops son of Dadon, Aristo— son of —.)

Anactorium: 30 minas. (Envoys: — son of Phormus, Arcus son of Tereus.)

Byzantium: 84 Lampsacene gold staters, 16 Attic silver drachmae. (The
money was brought by the Byzantine delegates ⟨to the synedrion of the
league based on Thebes⟩ Cercinus son of Hirotimus, Ag— son of
Deloptichus, Dionysius son of Hiraeon.)

Athenodorus son of Dionysius, of Tenedos, proxenos of the Boeotians:
1,000 drachmae.

16

In the archonship of Nicolaus

Alyzea: a further 30 minas. (Brought by the Alyzean envoys Theo—
son of Alexander, Dion son of Poly—.)

20

In the archonship of Agisinicus

Byzantium contributed a further 500 Lampsacene gold staters towards
the war which the Boeotians were fighting for the shrine at Delphi. (Brought
by the delegates Sosis son of Caratichus, Parmeniscus son of Pyramus.)

Partly restored, but there are no uncertainties apart from the gaps shown. The list is
apparently complete.

The cult of Apollo at Delphi was administered by the Delphic Amphictyony, an organisation in which central Greek peoples predominated. Thebes, in her rise to power in the
370's and 360's, came to control the Amphictyony, and attempted to use it for political
purposes. At her prompting, the Amphictyony decided to fine Sparta for her occupation of
the Theban acropolis in 382, and Phocis, the people living in the immediate vicinity of Delphi,
for cultivating the sacred land of Cirrha (a small but fertile plain just below Delphi and
visible from it). Both refused to pay; and when the Amphictyony threatened to confiscate
Phocian territory the Phocians, under Philomelus, seized Delphi (probably in 356; but some
date it a year later). After a winter of propaganda, and some preliminary skirmishing, the
Amphictyonic Council declared a Sacred War against Phocis. Phocis was supported by Sparta
(as another victim of the Amphictyons' anger), Athens (friendly to Sparta and hostile to
Thebes), and some other Peloponnesian cities; most of the central and northern Greek
peoples joined in the war on the Theban side. The Phocians controlled Delphi, and in due
course they yielded to temptation and used the temple treasures to finance their armies: this
inscription records gifts made to the Theban side. Byzantium, now outside the Second
Athenian League, showed her hostility to Athens by sending money to Thebes; Tenedos was
consistently loyal to Athens, but an individual citizen who was proxenos (cf. commentary on
no. 5) of Boeotia sent a contribution. The war continued until 346: Philip of Macedon was
first brought in on the Amphictyons' side in 353; in the winter of 347/6 a counter-revolution
brought back to power Phalaecus, a Phocian general who had been deposed for using the
temple treasures to finance his army; and he hoped (and Philip did not openly deny) that
Philip might be persuaded to change sides and support Phocis. Philip kept the Greeks in
suspense for as long as possible: when he did make it clear that he was still going to support

Thebes, resistance was no longer practicable, and Phocis had to capitulate. In 352 Philip had gained control of Thessaly, and therefore of Thessaly's two votes in the Amphictyonic Council; in 346 Phocis was expelled from the Amphictyony and was required to repay what she had taken from the temple treasuries, and her two votes in the Amphictyonic Council were given to Macedon.

The exact dates of the Boeotian archons are not known. The word "stater" denotes the standard coin of a state, irrespective of its value in terms of the units listed in the Introduction, p.viii: it was particularly used of the gold and electrum coins of Asia Minor.

9

Athens honours Bosporan Kings, 346

(IG ii² 212, SIG³ 206, Tod 167)

1   FOR SPARTOCUS, PAERISADES, APOLLONIUS, SONS OF LEUCON.

3   IN THE ARCHONSHIP OF THEMISTOCLES ⟨347/6⟩; IN THE EIGHTH PRYTANY, OF AEGEIS; WHEN LYSIMACHUS SON OF SOSIDEMUS, OF ACHARNAE, WAS SECRETARY; THEOPHILUS OF HALIMUS WAS CHAIRMAN; Androtion son of Andron, of Gargettus, proposed:—

8   Concerning what Spartocus and Paerisades have written and what the envoys who have come from them report: reply to them that the people of Athens praises Spartocus and Paerisades, because they are good men and promise to the people of Athens that they will take care of the dispatch of corn as their father did and will perform enthusiastically any service that the people requires; and the envoys shall report to them that if they do this they will not fail in any ⟨request⟩ from the people of Athens.

20   Since they grant to the Athenians the privileges which Satyrus and Leucon granted, Spartocus and Paerisades shall have the privileges which the people granted to Satyrus and Leucon; and crown each of them ⟨regularly⟩ at the Great Panathenaea with a gold crown of 1,000 drachmae: the athlothetae shall make the crowns in the year before the Great Panathe- naea, in accordance with the decree of the people previously voted for Leucon; and it shall be proclaimed that the people of Athens crowns Spartocus and Paerisades the sons of Leucon for their virtue and good- will towards the people of Athens; and since they ⟨offer to⟩ dedicate their crowns to Athena Polias, the athlothetae shall dedicate the crowns in the temple, with the inscription:

Spartocus and Paerisades sons of Leucon
dedicated ⟨these⟩ to Athena
on being crowned by the people of Athens.

The money for the crowns shall ⟨normally⟩ be given to the <u>athlothetae</u> by the treasurer of the people from the fund allocated to the people for expenditure on decrees; but for the present the <u>apodectae</u> shall provide the money from ⟨what they would allocate to⟩ the stratiotic fund.

44 The secretary of the council shall record this decree on a stone <u>stele</u> and erect it near that of Satyrus and Leucon, and for the inscription the treasurer of the people shall provide 30 drachmae.

49 Praise the envoys Sosis and Theodisius, because they take care of those visiting the Bosporus from Athens, and invite them to hospitality in the <u>prytaneum</u> tomorrow.

53 Concerning the money due to the sons of Leucon: in order that they may obtain it, the <u>proedri</u> to whose lot it falls to preside in the assembly on the eighteenth shall raise the question immediately after the religious business, that they may obtain the money and have no complaints against the people of Athens.

59 Provide the ships' officers for whom Spartocus and Paerisades ask: the envoys shall record the names of the ships' officers they take with the secretary of the council; and those who are recorded shall be doing their duty ⟨as Athenian citizens if they⟩ do what good they can for the sons of Leucon.

65 Polyeuctus son of Timocrates, of Crioa, proposed:—

66 In other respects in accordance with Androtion; but crown also Apollonius son of Leucon from the same ⟨fund?⟩.

The <u>stele</u> is complete, and the text is largely intact.

The Bosporan kingdom was based on the Cimmerian Bosporus (the Crimea), and embraced a wide area to the north of the Black Sea: the Spartocid dynasty ruled from 438/7 for more than three centuries. Seleucus and Satyrus I ruled (jointly until Seleucus' death in 393/2) from 433/2 to 389/8, and Leucon I from then until 349/8. Leucon's two eldest sons, Spartocus II and Paerisades I, succeeded as joint kings on his death. Spartocus died in 344/3, leaving Paerisades as sole king: he lived until 311/0. Athens had imported corn from the Black Sea (cf. paragraph beginning at 8) since the sixth century, and therefore went to some trouble to maintain good relations with this kingdom, as with the Thracian kingdom on the European shores of the Hellespont, through which the corn ships sailed (cf. no. 2). The Bosporan kingdom normally levied an export duty of $3\frac{1}{3}$% on corn, but one of the privileges granted to Athens (cf. paragraph beginning at 20) was exemption from this duty: Athens responded by conferring on the kings honorary citizenship and ateleia (freedom from the obligations of citizenship: cf. commentary on no. 5), and the regular award of a gold crown at the Great Panathenaea; and in this decree, issued not long after the death of Leucon, she confirms these privileges for the new kings, promises prompt attention to a debt due to the kingdom, and gives the Bosporans the right to recruit ships' officers in Athens.

The Panathenaea was a festival of Athena, and one of the major national festivals of Athens: it was celebrated annually in Hecatombaeon (i), and every fourth year more lavishly as the Great Panathenaea: to be regularly awarded crowns at this festival was flattery of a very high order. The crowns themselves were to be very sumptuous, costing 1,000 drachmae each: this is the highest figure found for a gold crown at this time. The athlothetae (ten men, one picked by lot from each tribe) served for the four years from one Great Panathenaea to the next: they were responsible for various aspects of the preparations for the festival, and it was natural that having these crowns made should have been added to their duties. Athena was worshipped with the cult title Polias as the patron deity of the city (cf. no.19, from Priene): an ancient, olive-wood statue of Athena was carried in procession at the Panathenaea, and at other times was housed in the Erechtheum, on the north side of the acropolis; that is presumably the temple in which these crowns were to be dedicated. On the financial mechanism underlying the end of the paragraph beginning at 20, see the Introduction, p. vii. On the referring of an item to the council for report to a later assembly (in the paragraph beginning at 53), see p. v: "the eighteenth" will have been 18 Elaphebolion (ix), the first available day after the Dionysia; this was in fact the first of two days devoted to the discussion of the Peace of Philocrates, which ended the state of war which had existed between Athens and Philip of Macedon since his occupation of Amphipolis in 357 (cf. commentary on no. 7); it had been hoped that Philip's envoys would arrive earlier, and that the peace could be discussed before the Dionysia, and it is possible that when this decree was carried that hope was still held, and that the postponed discussion of the peace terms in fact displaced the discussion of the debt to the Bosporans from 18 Elaphebolion. On the amendment with which the inscription ends, see the Introduction, p. vi. On Androtion, the author of the original decree, see no. 5 with commentary; Polyeuctus, the author of the amendment, and his father Timocrates appear in the late 350's and early 340's as enemies of Demosthenes.

Athens honours Arybbas the Molossian, c. 342

(IG ii² 226, SIG³ 228, Tod 173)

1   GODS.

    OF ARYBBAS.

    (lacuna)

3   . . . Since the citizenship awarded to his father and grandfather and the other privileges are available also to him and his descendants and have been confirmed:care shall be taken of Arybbas, that he may suffer no injustice, by the council for the time being and the generals for the time being and any other Athenian who may be present.   He shall have <the right of> access to both council and people whenever he asks, and the prytany in office shall take care that he obtains access.

19   The secretary of the council shall record this decree on a stone stele and erect it on the acropolis: for the inscription of the stele the treasurer of the people shall provide 30 drachmae from the fund allocated to the people for expenditure on decrees.

28   Invite Arybbas to dinner in the prytaneum tomorrow; and also invite those who have come with Arybbas to hospitality in the prytaneum tomorrow.

33   Deal also with the other matters of which Arybbas speaks.

35   In other respects in accordance with the council; but if any one kills Arybbas or any of the sons of Arybbas by a violent death, he shall be liable to the same penalty as for <killing> any other Athenian. Also the generals in office shall take care that Arybbas and his sons recover their ancestral realm.

48   (There follow three representations of crowns, in the first two of which are preserved:)

Olympic ⟨Games⟩	Pythian ⟨Games⟩
with a ⟨chariot	with a ⟨chariot
drawn by⟩	drawn by⟩
full ⟨grown horses⟩	full ⟨grown horses⟩

Except at the beginning, what survives of the text is almost intact.

Arybbas had been king of the Molossi, in Epirus (north-western Greece). His father Alcetas and elder brother Neoptolemus joined the Second Athenian League, probably in 375, and were included in the list of members on no.1. On Alcetas' death Arybbas challenged Neoptolemus' claim to succeed him: they ruled jointly until Neoptolemus' death, after which Arybbas ruled alone. Olympias, a daughter of Neoptolemus, was married to Philip of Macedon (and bore him a son, Alexander the Great, and a daughter, Cleopatra), and about 342 Philip intervened in the kingdom, expelling Arybbas in favour of Olympias' brother Alexander; Arybbas fled to Athens, appealing for protection and restoration to his kingdom. By this time, Demosthenes' policy of distrusting Philip and of watching for a pretext to renew the war against him (on the Peace of Philocrates, in 346, cf. the commentary on no. 9) was gaining general acceptance in Athens, and Arybbas was favourably received. In fact Athens did not restore Arybbas to Epirus. Philip was persuaded in 337 to divorce Olympias and take a wife from the Macedonian nobility; in the following year, to placate Olympias' family, he arranged to marry Cleopatra, his daughter by Olympias, to Olympias' brother Alexander; on the day of the wedding, Philip was assassinated; his Macedonian wife had not borne him a son, and Alexander the Great, his son by Olympias, was able to succeed to the throne of Macedon. The relationships mentioned in this note may be shown as follows (men's names are given in capital letters):—

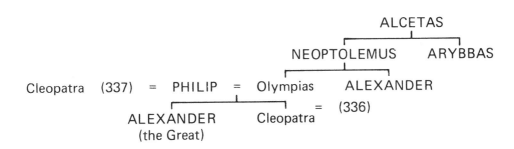

On the invocation of the gods at the beginning of the inscription, see the Introduction, p. vi. The privileges specified in the paragraph beginning at 3 — protection from injustice, and the right of access to the council and assembly — were commonly granted to foreigners honoured by the Athenians. Notice that Arybbas, as an honorary citizen of Athens, is invited to "dinner", while those who those have come with him are invited to "hospitality" (cf. commentary on no. 3). The paragraph beginning at 33 is the end of the council's <u>probouleuma</u>, which offered conventional honours and privileges to Arybbas, but was not prepared to venture a recommendation on the more controversial questions of protecting Arybbas and his sons from assassination and restoring him to his kingdom: these questions were discussed in the assembly, whose decision is recorded in the form of an amendment to the <u>probouleuma</u>; the name of the man who proposed the amendment has been omitted (cf. the Introduction, pp. v — vi). The <u>stele</u> on which the text was inscribed was an elaborate one, with sculptured reliefs above and below the text: Tod suggests that Arybbas probably had to add a sizeable contribution to the 30 drachmae voted by the state (paragraph beginning at 19).

Athens honours Elaeus, 340

(IG ii² 228, SIG³ 255, Tod 174)

1   In the archonship of Nicomachus ⟨341/0⟩ ; in the seventh prytany, of
     Pandionis; on the twenty-ninth of the prytany; the question was put by
     Aristomachus of Oeum, ⟨chairman⟩ of the proedri; Onesippus of Araphen
     was secretary; resolved by the people; Hippostratus son of Etearchides,
     of Pallene, proposed:—

8   Grant to the people of Elaeus the same things as the people has voted
     for the people of the Chersonese; and the general Chares shall take care
     of them in the same way, so that the people of Elaeus may rightly and
     justly retain their own ⟨possessions⟩ and live with the Athenians in the
     Chersonese.

16   Invite the men from Elaeus to dinner in the prytaneum tomorrow.

The text is largely intact, and there are no uncertainties.

   In 353/2 Cersobleptes, when under pressure from Philip of Macedon, had
decided to adhere to his alliance with Athens, and had ceded to Athens all the cities
of the Chersonese except Cardia (on the isthmus); and the Athenians had sent out cleruchs
(settlers who retained their Athenian citizenship) to ensure that the Hellespont was kept
safe for Athenian shipping (cf. commentary on no. 2). In the spring of 346, while the Peace
of Philocrates was being negotiated in Athens (cf. commentary on no. 9) Cersobleptes was
defeated by Philip, and was reduced to the status of a vassal king: his attempt to join the
Second Athenian League in time to be included in the Peace of Philocrates failed. In 342
Philip intervened in eastern Thrace again, and deposed Cersobleptes: Athens, to protect her
interests, sent out reinforcements to her cleruchies, accompanied by an army under the
command of Diopithes. Diopithes came into conflict with Cardia, named in the Peace of
Philocrates as an ally of Philip; in Athens, in 341, his actions were condemned by some but
defended by Demosthenes; further incidents involving Athens and Macedon occurred in the
region of the Chersonese and elsewhere, and Philip protested to Athens; in the summer of
340 (rather later than this decree) Philip began his unsuccessful attempt to capture Perinthus
(on the Propontis) and Byzantium, and after Philip had captured a fleet of Athenian merchant
ships Athens declared war. For the sequel, cf. commentary on no.12. In this simple decree
the city of Elaeus (near the south-western tip of the Chersonese; a member of the Second
Athenian League — cf. no.1 — which remained consistently loyal to Athens) is promised the
same protection by Athens and cooperation with the Athenian cleruchs as has been granted
to the other cities of the Chersonese.

   For the earlier career of Chares, cf. commentary on no. 3. Demosthenes' defence of
Diopithes in 341 was successful enough for Chares to be sent to reinforce him; the merchant

fleet which Philip captured was awaiting Chares' return from discussions with the Persians to escort it through the Hellespont; subsequently the Byzantines distrusted him and refused to admit him, and he was superseded in the north-east by Phocion. The invitation to "dinner" (paragraph beginning at 16) suggests that the envoys from Elaeus were men who had already received honorary Athenian citizenship (cf. commentary on nos. 3 and 10).

12

Athens honours Tenedos, 340/39

(IG ii² 233, SIG³ 256, Tod 175)

1   In the archonship of Theophrastus ⟨340/39⟩ ; resolved by the people; Cecropis was in prytany; on the eighth of the prytany; the question was put by S—, ⟨chairman⟩ of the proedri; Aspetus son of Demostratus, of Cytherrus, was secretary; Callicrates son of Charopides, of Lamptrae, proposed:—

5   Concerning what the men from Tenedos say: praise the people of Tenedos for its virtue and goodwill towards the people of Athens and towards the allies, and for the help it has given both in former times and now . . .

10   (A section follows in which it is impossible to reconstruct a continuous text, but a few extracts can be given:) . . . so that the people of Tenedos may recover the money which it lent to the people of Athens in the year of Theophrastus' archonship . . . for assistance . . . the people shall resolve . . . ⟨the year⟩ after Theophrastus ⟨' archonship⟩ . . . the voted syntaxis . . . and for the current administration . . .

22   . . . they shall convey to Tenedos in the year after Theophrastus' archonship; this shall apply to them until they have conveyed all the money; and during this time it shall be forbidden for any general or for any one else to exact any money or anything else, and also during this time for the delegates to assess anything ⟨from Tenedos⟩, until the people of Tenedos has recovered all the money which it lent; so that in future it shall be known to the allies and to any one else who is well disposed towards the people of Athens that the people of Athens takes just care of those of the allies who do what is to the advantage of the people of Athens and the allies.

35   Praise the people of Tenedos and crown it with a gold crown of 1,000

drachmae for its virtue and goodwill towards the people of Athens and
the allies. Praise also Aratus, the delegate of Tenedos, and crown him
with an olive crown. Praise also . . . the delegates of . . .

Two fragments survive which do not join; neither extends over much more than half of the
line-length (which is established by the opening formulae and by lines 35 sqq.).

In the summer of 340 Philip of Macedon sent a fleet into the Propontis, and laid seige
to Perinthus, which was inclining towards Athens; half his forces were detached to besiege
Byzantium when that city sent help to Perinthus; Athens formally declared war when Philip
captured a fleet of Athenian merchant ships (cf. commentary on no.11). The appearance of
Philip's forces here alarmed Persia and many Aegean cities, including those which had gained
their independence by the Social War of 356—355 (cf. commentary on nos. 3 and 6), and
Athens received considerable support for the defence of the besieged cities: in the spring of
339, having made no progress, Philip tricked the Athenian commanders into letting him with-
draw his forces. This decree is probably to be assigned to the summer of 339, after Philip had
withdrawn. Tenedos is an island lying a short way outside the Aegean entrance to the
Hellespont: it had a long record of loyalty to Athens, and was one of the first states to join
the Second League (cf. list in no.1, section beginning at 79); in the crisis of 340/39 it helped
Athens by lending money, and this decree provides for the repayment of the money and
stipulates that Tenedos is to be free from all impositions until the repayment has been
completed.

This inscription is our last evidence for the functioning of the Second Athenian League,
which passed out of existence when Philip organised the Greeks in the League of Corinth
(cf. no.13): it shows that the member states still sent delegates to the League's synedrion,
and that the synedrion assessed the syntaxeis to be collected from the members. Aratus, the
delegate from Tenedos, seems to have played a large part in securing his city's support for
Athens. Like the Bosporan kings (cf. no. 9 with commentary), Tenedos was awarded an
elaborate gold crown, at the maximum price spent on crowns at this time.

13

**Peace of the Greeks with Philip of Macedon,
and Establishment of the League of Corinth, 338/7**

(IG ii² 236, SIG³ 260, Tod 177)

1   Oath:—

I swear by Zeus, by Earth, by Sun, by Poseidon, by Athena, by Ares and
by all the gods and goddesses that I shall abide by the peace and shall not
break the agreement made with Philip of Macedon; nor shall I take up
arms with harmful intent either by land or by sea against those who abide
by the oaths; nor shall I with warlike intent take any city or fortress or

harbour belonging to those participating in the peace, by any craft or contrivance; nor shall I overthrow the kingdom of Philip and his descendants, or the constitution which each ⟨member state⟩ had when it took the oaths to the peace; nor shall I do anything contrary to these agreements myself nor allow any one else to do so as far as I am able; and if any one does commit any breach of the peace with regard to these agreements, I shall assist as called upon by those who are wronged, and shall fight against those transgressing the common peace as decided by the common synedrion and as called upon by the hegemon; and I shall not give up . . .

22   (lacuna)

24

. . .	5
[demos of Corcyra	2]
[Thes] salians	10
[Magnesians near Thessaly]	2
[Phthotid Achaeans	2]
[Is] landers	1
[demos of Samothrace and] Thasos	2
[Aetolians	5]
[Acarnan] ians	2
Ambraci [ots	1]
— from Thrace and —	—
Phocians	3
Locrians	3
[Dorians, Oet] aeans, Malians, [Aeni- anians, Agr] aeans, Dolopians	5
[Athamanians and Pe] rrhaebians	2
[demos of Zacynthus] and Cephallenia	3

Two fragments: the first gives the oath sworn by the Greek states to Philip (rather less than half of each line survives, but comparison with other documents makes the restoration fairly safe); the second is part of a list of members with (apparently) the number of delegates each sent to the synedrion (restorations are enclosed in square brackets: details may be disputed, but the nature of the list is clear).

At the Amphictyonic Council in the autumn of 340, Aeschines, one of Athens' representatives, tried to distract attention from tactless behaviour towards Thebes by Athens, by drawing attention to the fact that the Amphissans, who had remarked on Athens' tactlessness, were themselves committing the greater offence of cultivating the sacred land of Cirrha (cf. commentary on no. 8). A Sacred War was declared against Amphissa: Thebes stood out; and Demosthenes, realising that Thebes was the one state of any substance between Athens and the power of Philip, contrived to keep Athens out of the war too. On his return from Perinthus in 339 (cf. commentary on nos. 11 and 12), Philip was given command of the Amphictyonic forces; and when his army came south Demosthenes negotiated an alliance with Thebes to resist him. In 338 he defeated Athens and Thebes at Chaeronea, and then toured Greece, to have his supremacy acknowledged by all cities except Sparta — which he ignored. In the winter of 338/7 he summoned representatives of the cities to Corinth, imposed on the Greeks a common peace treaty, after the manner of the peace of 386 (cf. commentary on no. 1) and its successors, and organised them in a league, the so-called League of Corinth, after the manner of the Second Athenian League (cf. no. 1 with commentary) and other Greek partisan leagues. He thus combined two traditions in Greek inter-state diplomacy: a peace treaty, to deal with current quarrels and to maintain a balance of weakness, and a league, which left the cities free in their internal affairs but in other respects united them under his leadership. The league then, at his prompting, voted for a crusade against the Persians, and appointed Philip to be its commander in the crusade: advance forces were sent out by Philip; and after his assassination (cf. commentary on no. 10) the crusade was undertaken in earnest by Alexander. For Alexander's enlargement of the league and dealings with it, see nos. 17—19 and 23 with commentary.

For the oath, cf. no. 7, lines 38 sqq., and for the organisation of the members in a synedrion and the publication of a list of members, cf. the prospectus of the Second Athenian League, no. 1. This copy of the text was found in Athens: its missing parts presumably included an Athenian decree accepting Philip's terms, and the oath sworn by Philip to the Greeks, to counterbalance the oath sworn by the Greeks to him. The undertaking of the Greeks includes a declaration of loyalty to the kingdom of Macedon in perpetuity; Macedon was not a member state with voting rights in the synedrion, but it was inevitable that Philip should be elected hegemon (executive officer) of the league, and it seems that in 336 Alexander, as the new king of Macedon, was recognised by the Greeks as succeeding to the position of hegemon as of right. In the list of members we have a novelty: the numbers given with the names of members or groups of members are apparently the numbers of voting delegates which each sent to the synedrion (probably determined in proportion to the forces which they put at the league's disposal): in the earlier Greek leagues each member state had had a single vote; but the federal constitution of Boeotia (where Philip had spent some years as a hostage) gave different voting strengths and military obligations to the different cities. The word demos, if correctly restored with the names of Corcyra, Samothrace and Zacynthus, was presumably inserted to stress that these states entered the league as democracies (cf. the list in no. 1).

Athens honours loyal Acarnanians, 337

(IG ii² 237, SIG³ 259, Tod 178)

1   In the archonship of Chaerondas ⟨338/7⟩ ; in the tenth prytany, of
    Pandionis; when Philip son of Antiphemus, of Eiresidae, was secretary;
    on 27 Thargelion (xi), on the third of the prytany; the question was put
    by — of Erchia, ⟨chairman⟩ of the proedri; resolved by the people;
    Hegesippus son of Hegesias, of Sunium, proposed:—

6   Concerning what is said by the Acarnanians Phormio and Carphinas,
    who have recently come, the people shall resolve:

8   Since Phormio and Carphinas, being ancestral friends of the people of
    Athens, maintain the goodwill towards the people of Athens which their
    ancestors handed down to them; and now have helped us with a military
    force and have been ranked with the Athenians under the command of
    the general: praise them for their virtue and crown each of them with a
    gold crown.

15 And since the Athenian people made Phormio the grandfather of Phormio
    and Carphinas an Athenian ⟨citizen⟩ , together with his descendants, and
    the decree by which the grant was made has been recorded on the acropolis,
    the award which the people made to their grandfather Phormio shall be
    valid for Phormio and Carphinas and their descendants. They shall choose
    the tribe, deme and phratry to which they wish to belong.

22 Praise also the other Acarnanians who have rendered assistance with
    Phormio and Carphinas; and they shall have, until they return ⟨home, the
    right⟩ to own whatever houses they wish, to live in Athens immune from
    the metic ⟨tax⟩, to give and receive justice on the same terms as Athenian
    ⟨citizens⟩, and to pay the eisphorae, if there are any, with the Athenian
    ⟨citizens⟩; and the council for the time being and the generals for the
    time being shall take care of them, that they suffer no injustice.

31 The secretary of the council shall record this decree on a stone stele and
    erect it on the acropolis; record also on the same stele the names of the
    Acarnanians, appending the city in Acarnania to which each belongs. For
    the inscription of the stele the treasurer of the people shall supply to the
    secretary of the council 30 drachmae from the people's fund for expendi-
    ture on decrees.

39 (There follow two representations of crowns, within which are inscribed:)

Phormio	Carphinas
⟨crowned by⟩	⟨crowned by⟩
the people	the people

The stele is almost complete, but its surface is badly worn. The first paragraph is largely restored (father and deme of the secretary suggested by G. A. Stamires; date in month and day in prytany very uncertain); in the next three paragraphs all but a few letters are legible; from line 22 to the end restoration is increasingly necessary.

Acarnania (on the west coast of Greece, immediately to the north of the Corinthian Gulf) had been well disposed towards Athens since the Athenian general Phormio had made himself very popular there in the 430's and 420's; it is presumably owing to a close association with him that the name Phormio passed into the family honoured here. Phormio and Carphinas appear to have brought a body of Acarnanians to fight with the Athenians against Philip at Chaeronea in 338 (cf. commentary on no.13); after the battle, in the course of his settlement of Greece, Philip occupied Acarnania and secured the exile of these men, who fled to Athens.

On Hegesippus, the author of the decree, see no. 4 with commentary. Unusually, the amount to be spent on the crowns has not been specified (cf. commentary on no. 9). On the tribes and demes, to which all Athenian citizens belonged, see the Introduction, p. iv; the phratries (brotherhoods) were older subdivisions of the Athenian people (originally each phratry had perhaps comprised one aristocratic clan and its dependants — but this is controversial), no longer of direct political significance, but still considered worth belonging to. Since membership both of the tribes and demes and of the phratries was hereditary, the elder Phormio must have failed to take up the citizenship voted to him. Foreigners resident in Athens were known as metics: unless specially privileged, they were not allowed to own land or houses, were subject to certain restrictions in the law courts, were required to pay a special poll tax, and, if rich enough to be liable to the property tax known as eisphora (a proportion of a man's declared property, levied, in each year when the state needed the money, on all those whose declared property was above a certain level), they paid at a higher rate than the citizens. Phormio and Carphinas are to be citizens, with all the rights of citizens; their fellow-exiles are given the right to own houses, equality with the citizens in the courts, and isoteleia, equality with the citizens in their financial obligations. (For a similar grant of privileges cf. no. 21).

Athenian Law against Tyranny, 336

(Hesp. xxi 1952, pp. 355–9, no. 5; SEG xii 87)

1   In the archonship of Phrynichus ⟨337/6⟩; in the ninth prytany, of
     Leontis; when Chaerestratus son of Aminias, of Acharnae, was secretary;
     the question was put by Menestratus of Aexone, ⟨chairman⟩ of the
     proedri; Eucrates son of Aristotimus, of Piraeus, proposed:—

5   For the good fortune of the people of Athens, the nomothetae shall
     resolve:

7   If any one rises against the people with tyrannical intent, or joins in
     setting up a tyranny, or overthrows the people of Athens or the demo-
     cracy at Athens:

10   Whoever kills any one who does any of these things shall go unpunished;

11   And it shall be forbidden for the members of the Council of the Areopagus,
     if the people or the democracy at Athens is overthrown, to go up on to
     the Areopagus and to sit in council and to deliberate about anything;
     and if, when the people or democracy at Athens has been overthrown,
     any of the members of the Council of the Areopagus does go up on to
     the Areopagus or sit in council or deliberate about anything, he shall
     lose his civic rights, both he and his descendants, and his property shall
     be confiscated, a tenth being dedicated to the goddess ⟨Athena⟩.

22   The secretary of the council shall record this law on two stone stelae,
     and shall place one at the entrance to the Areopagus on the way to the
     council chamber and the other in the assembly. For the inscription of
     the stelae the treasurer of the people shall provide 20 drachmae from the
     people's fund for expenditure on decrees.

For once the inscribed surface is intact, and every letter can be read: there are a few
"misprints".

     The Council of the Areopagus (so called from the hill where it met) comprised all living
ex-archons, except any who had lost their civic rights for misconduct in office. The archons

were the most important officials of early Athens, and the ex-archons in the Areopagus had great prestige and (through their judicial functions and their supervision of magistrates) considerable power. Between the middle of the sixth century and the middle of the fifth, the archonship declined into a routine office, and in 462/1 Ephialtes deprived the Areopagus of the duties which gave it political power. For the next century or more the Areopagus was unimportant politically, though at times it figured in discussions of what the Good Old Days had been like. In the 340's, however, the Areopagus began to appear again in political contexts, normally to the advantage of Demosthenes. About 343, when Aeschines was elected to defend Athenian control of the sanctuary of Apollo on the island of Delos against complaints made by the Delians to the Amphictyonic Council, the Areopagus managed to have the election quashed and Demosthenes' associate Hyperides elected in his place (his defence of Athens' claims was in fact successful). About 340 a man called Antiphon, deleted from the register of citizens in 346, was brought before the assembly by Demosthenes on a charge of planning to burn Athens' dockyards for Philip; Aeschines defended him, and he was acquitted; but the Areopagus then managed to have the case reopened, and Antiphon was convicted and executed. In 338, in the panic following Philip's victory at Chaeronea (cf. commentary on no.13), some Athenians wanted the chief command to go to the extremist Charidemus (a Euboean who had settled in Athens and had received Athenian citizenship: at an earlier stage in his career he had served as a mercenary commander to the Thracian prince Cersobleptes — on whom cf. commentary on nos. 2 and 11), but the Areopagus was able to ensure that the command went to Phocion (a general whose political sympathies were with Aeschines and those who wished to coopérate with Philip, but who was widely trusted). Attitudes changed rapidly in Athens, according to whether Philip's last action seemed favourable or unfavourable to Athens. In a period of anti-Macedonian feelings, various men were prosecuted and condemned for cowardice or treachery at Chaeronea, and some of these cases seem to have been heard by the Areopagus. It is not clear how far the Areopagus was simply making representations to the assembly, and getting its way, and how far its constitutional powers had been enhanced: in the trials after Chaeronea it seems to have been exercising judicial power of a kind which it had lost in 462/1; in all the other instances it could have achieved its results simply by making representations to an assembly which was persuaded to give it a favourable hearing, though in the case of Antiphon we are told that the Areopagus was using powers given to it by a decree of Demosthenes. At any rate, Demosthenes' opponents were worried by the use he was making of the Areopagus; and early in the summer of 336, when Philip's preparations for a crusade against the Persians (which would take him and his army far away from Athens) led to a revival of pro-Macedonian feeling, this law was proposed, threatening the Areopagus with suspension if the Athenian democracy was overthrown. After this law was carried, something remained of the Areopagus' new prestige, though in the end Demosthenes' trust in the Areopagus recoiled on him. In 324 Alexander's treasurer Harpalus fled with as many soldiers and as much money as he could bring: at first he was refused admission to Athens; but when he came as a suppliant, with no soldiers and 700 talents, he was admitted but placed under arrest and the money was deposited on the acropolis. After a while it was found that half the money had disappeared, and soon afterwards Harpalus himself escaped: on the proposal of Demosthenes the Areopagus was ordered to investigate the matter; but when it published its list of offenders the name of Demosthenes headed the list.

This is the only text in this collection which was enacted by the Athenians' more complicated legislative procedure, nomothesia (cf. the Introduction, p.v). The proposer will have valued the extra importance which this procedure gave to his measure; and in all probability the consolidated law code of the end of the fifth century contained a law against tyranny which, it could be argued, could only be altered or added to by this procedure. The prescript (paragraph beginning at 1) is closely modelled on the prescripts of decrees, and shows that the nomothetae were presided over by their own subcommittee of proedri. Various laws against tyranny are known from Athens: they all share the disadvantage that they could only be enforced if an attempt to overthrow the democratic constitution failed, but the enactment of this law in 336 may nevertheless have been effective as a warning that not every one approved of the revival of the Areopagus as a politically active body. The surviving stele is a large one, with a sculptured relief (showing Demos, the People, crowned by Democratia) above the text: 20 drachmae is a surprisingly low allowance for two copies (cf. the Introduction, p. iii).

16

Athens allows Citian Merchants to found a Temple, 333

(IG ii² 337, SIG³ 280, Tod 189)

1   GODS.

2   In the archonship of Nicocrates ⟨333/2⟩; in the first prytany, of Aegeis; the question was put by Theophilus of Phegaea, ⟨chairman⟩ of the proedri; resolved by the council; Antidotus son of Apollodorus, of Sypalettus, proposed:—

9   Concerning what the Citians say about the foundation of the temple to Aphrodite: the council shall resolve that the proedri to whose lot it falls to preside in the next assembly shall bring them forward and deal with the business, and put to the people the opinion of the council, that it seems good to the council that concerning the foundation of the temple the people should listen to the Citians, and to any one else, from among the Athenians, who wishes ⟨to speak⟩, and should decide as it thinks best.

26   In the archonship of Nicocrates ⟨333/2⟩; in the second prytany, of Pandionis; the question was put by Phanostratus of Philaidae, ⟨chairman⟩ of the proedri; Lycurgus son of Lycophron, of Butadae, proposed:—

33   Since it has appeared that the Citian merchants are making a legitimate request in asking the people for ⟨the right⟩ to acquire land on which they propose to erect a temple of Aphrodite; the people shall resolve to grant to the Citian merchants ⟨the right⟩ to acquire land on which to erect their temple of Aphrodite, in the same way as the Egyptians have erected their temple of Isis.

The stele is complete, and only three letters of the text have been lost.

Non-citizens, unless specially privileged, were not allowed to own land in Attica (cf. commentary on no. 14): the merchants from Citium, in Cyprus, therefore required special permission to build their temple of Aphrodite, the patron goddess of Cyprus. There was presumably a community of Citians resident in Athens as metics, and the temple will have provided for the religious needs both of them and of other Citians paying short-term visits to Athens.

On the invocation of the gods at the beginning of the inscription, see the Introduction, p. vi. The inscription is unusually revealing on the procedure by which the assembly's decree was enacted: the three paragraphs beginning at line 2 comprise the probouleuma, in which the council placed the Citians' request on the agenda of the assembly and, rather than make a positive recommendation, simply left the assembly to make up its own mind; the last two paragraphs give us the resulting decree of the assembly, noting a precedent and granting the request (cf. the Introduction, p. v). The absence of a clause ordering the publication of the decree suggests (but does not prove, as the Athenians tended to be careless about such matters) that the stele was set up by the Citians at their own expense. The author of the assembly's decree was Lycurgus, who was an associate of Demosthenes in the early 330's, and later exercised a general financial control in Athens (cf. commentary on no. 21).

17

Documents concerning Tyranny at Eresus, 332 and after

(IG XII.ii 526, OGIS 8, Tod 191)

(The inscription contains parts of seven distinct documents, which I designate by roman numerals.)

I

1   . . . besieged, and he rebuilt the acropolis, exacted 20,000 staters from
       the citizens, plundered the Greeks, destroyed the altars of Zeus Philippius,
       and waged war on Alexander and the Greeks; he deprived the citizens of
       their arms and shut them all out of the city; he seized their wives and
       children, confined them in the acropolis, and exacted 3,200 staters ⟨ransom⟩;
       with the pirates he plundered and burned the city and the shrines, and
       joined in burning the bodies of citizens; and, finally, on arrival in the
       presence of Alexander he falsely slandered the citizens:

15   Judge him on a secret ballot, on oath, for the penalty of death; and, if he
       is condemned to death, when Agonippus has made his counter-proposal,

decide the second issue, ⟨that is,⟩ in what way he should die;

20 And if after Agonippus has met with justice any one brings back any of the sons of Agonippus, or proposes or ⟨as presiding officer⟩ puts forward a proposal for their return or the restoration of their property, he shall be cursed, both himself and his family, and shall be liable to everything else enjoined by law for those who overthrow the stele concerning the tyrants and their descendants.

26 Offer a prayer immediately in the assembly, that it may be well with him who in judging supports the city and with a just ⟨vote⟩ , but otherwise with those cast their vote contrary to justice.

30 Vote taken: 883 ⟨votes were cast⟩ ; of these 7 were for acquittal, the rest for conviction.

II

33 Resolved by the people:—

33 Concerning the report of the envoys sent to Alexander and the edict sent by Alexander: Since Heroides son of Terticon son of Heraeus and Agesimenes son of Hermesideus ⟨son of Hermon⟩ , the descendants of the former tyrants, have arrived in Alexander's presence and have reported to him that they are willing to submit to justice among the people;

41 For good fortune the people shall resolve: Since Ag⟨esimenes?⟩ . . .

III

42 . . . deprived of their arms and shut them all out of the city; he seized their wives and children, confined them in the acropolis, and exacted 2,300 staters ⟨ransom⟩ ; with the pirates he plundered and burned the city and the shrines, and he joined in burning the bodies of citizens;

56 Judge him on a secret ballot in accordance with the edict of King Alexander and the laws; and, if he is condemned to death, when Eurysilaus has made his counter-proposal, make the second decision by show of hands, ⟨that is,⟩ in what way he should die.

68   The city shall appoint ten advocates, who shall swear by Apollo <u>Lyceus</u> that as advocates they will serve the city as best they can . . .

74   (<u>lacuna</u>)

76   . . . that if he is just and supports the city and the laws with a just ⟨vote⟩ it may be well with him and his descendants, but otherwise with any one who judges against the laws and justice.

IV

84   The citizens who are to be jurors shall swear:—

87   I shall render justice, in matters lying within the laws, in accordance with the laws; in other matters, conscientiously, as well and as justly as I am able; and if he is convicted I shall punish him rightly and justly. That I shall do this I swear by Zeus and Sun.

V

97   OF PHILIP ⟨ARRHIDAEUS⟩.

98   The judgments delivered on the exiles by Alexander shall stand as valid: those whom he condemned to exile shall be exiled, but shall not be liable to extradition.

VI

104   <u>Prytanis</u> Melidorus. King Antigonus to the council and people of Eresus, greetings.

108   Your envoys have appeared before us and have spoken with us, saying that the people has received the letter from us, which we wrote concerning the sons of Agonippus, and that it has enacted a decree, which ⟨the envoys⟩ read to us . . .

117   (<u>lacuna</u>)

121   . . . meeting with Alexander. Farewell.

VII

123   Resolved by the people:—

123   Concerning what the council said in its probouleuma, or the resolution
or the revised resolution of the council, and the men who were elected
have produced all that was written against the tyrants, those who resided
in the city ⟨under their rule⟩, and their descendants, and have submitted
them with the documents to the assembly:

127   Since previously King Alexander sent an edict in which he ordered the
people of Eresus to hold a trial of Agonippus and Eurysilaus, to decide
what should be done with them; and the people hearing the edict set up
a court in accordance with the laws, which condemned Agonippus and
Eurysilaus to death, rendered their descendants liable to the law on the
stele, and ordered their property to be sold in accordance with the law;

136   And when Alexander sent a letter about the sons of Apollodorus, and
about Apollodorus' brothers Hermon and Heraeus, who had previously
been tyrants of the city, and their descendants, that the people should
decide whether or not they should ⟨be allowed to⟩ return, the people
hearing the edict set up a court for them in accordance with the law and
the edict of king Alexander, and when speeches had been made on both
sides decided that the law against the tyrants should be valid and that
they should be exiled from the city;

146   The people shall resolve: that the law against the tyrants written on the
old stele, the edicts of the kings against them, the decrees formerly
inscribed by our forbears, and the votes against the tyrants, shall be
valid against the tyrants, those who resided in the city ⟨under their rule⟩,
and their descendants. If in contravention of these any of the tyrants or
of those who resided in the city ⟨under their rule⟩ or of their descendants
is caught setting foot on the territory of Eresus . . . the people shall
deliberate . . .

Two fragments of stone: it used to be believed that the two were from a single large stele but
A.J. Heisserer has shown that they are from separate stelae and that there was also another
stele containing "the law against the tyrants". I continue to print the text in the order of the
older editions, but it should be noticed that lines 42-74 are not from the same stele as the rest
of the dossier, and that lines 76-84 do not belong to document III (and may belong to document II). Where a translation is given the text is sufficiently nearly intact for there to be no
doubt about the general sense or about most of the particular restorations.

Eresus, on the island of Lesbos, was a member of the Second Athenian League (cf. list in
no. 1) which left the league as a result of the Social War (cf. commentary on nos. 3 and 6).
The sequence of events behind this inscription is not certain but may be as follows. Soon after
the Social War three brothers, Hermon, Heraeus and Apollodorus, seized power as joint

tyrants, to be expelled, perhaps with the help of Philip of Macedon (cf. paragraph beginning at 136, and the reference to Zeus Philippius in the paragraph beginning at 1). Early in Alexander's reign two new tyrants seized power, Agonippus and Eurysilaus; in 334, after his victory on the Granicus, Alexander expelled them; but in 333 they supported Memnon of Rhodes (the Persians' mercenary commander, who was beginning a successful campaign in Alexander's rear, but died before he was able to cause serious trouble for Alexander), were reinstated, and treated their opponents savagely. In 332 the city was liberated again, and the tyrants were sent to Alexander in Egypt: he sent them back to Eresus with a letter containing an edict, in accordance with which a court was set up to try them and they were condemned to death (documents I, III, IV; cf. VII, paragraph beginning at 127). Alexander mentioned in his letter that the surviving members of the family which had held the earlier tyranny had come to him and wanted to be reinstated in Eresus: a court was set up to consider their case, and decided to maintain the sentence of exile passed on the tyrants and their descendants (document II; cf. VII, paragraph beginning at 136). After Alexander's death, in 323, the throne was nominally shared by his half-brother Philip Arrhidaeus and his son Alexander, while the generals fought for real power: document V is an edict issued in the name of Philip Arrhidaeus, confirming the sentences on the tyrants. Of the generals, Antigonus the One-Eyed, who at Alexander's death held a command in Asia Minor, extended his power in Asia, and in due course claimed the title of king for himself. The sons of Agonippus appealed to him to reinstate them in Eresus, and he sent a letter to Eresus (document VI), as a result of which the whole history of the case was reviewed, and Eresus once more confirmed its earlier decisions (document VII).

The word "stater" denotes the standard coin of a state, irrespective of its value in terms of the units listed in the Introduction, p. viii: unless a total ransom of 5,500 staters was oddly divided between Agonippus and Eurysilaus we must assume that there is an error either in the paragraph beginning at 1 or in the paragraph beginning at 42, and that the same sum of money should have been mentioned in each place (in the Greek text the sum is spelled out in words on each occasion). The stele mentioned in various places (in the last paragraph as "the old stele") will have contained the law enacted when the first tyrants were expelled (for laws against tyrants in Athens, cf. no. 15 with commentary). In document VI, the prytanis mentioned in the paragraph beginning at 104 will have been the eponymous magistrate (cf. the Introduction, p. vii, and nos. 18, 23) in whose year of office the letter from Antigonus arrived. Technically, Eresus will have joined the League of Corinth when first liberated by Alexander (cf. commentary on no. 18): one rule of the league was that member states should retain the constitution they had when they joined (cf. no. 13), and this will have provided Alexander with the excuse, if he was conscious that he needed one, for his subsequent orders to Eresus.

18

Alexander restores Chian Exiles, 334 or 332

(SIG³ 283, Tod 192)

1 In the prytany of Disitheus; from King Alexander to the people of Chios:—

2 All the exiles from Chios shall return, and the constitution in Chios shall

be a democracy. Nomographi shall be chosen to write and correct the laws, so that there shall be nothing in conflict with the democracy or with the return of the exiles. What is corrected or recorded shall be reported to Alexander.

8   The Chians shall provide twenty manned triremes at their own expense, and these shall sail as far as the rest of the Greek fleet sails with us.

10   Of those who betrayed the city to the barbarians, those who have got away shall be exiled from all the cities participating in the peace, and shall be liable to extradition in accordance with the resolution of the Greeks: those who have been caught shall be brought and judged in the synedrion of the Greeks.

15   If there is any dispute between the returned ⟨exiles⟩ and those ⟨who stayed⟩ in the city, judgment on this shall be in our own court.

17   Until the Chians are reconciled, they shall have a garrison from King Alexander, as large as is sufficient: this shall be maintained by the Chians.

The stele is intact, and only a few letters are lost.

Chios supported Alexander at the beginning of his campaign against the Persians. It was betrayed to Memnon by members of an oligarchic faction in 333, and recovered by the Macedonians in 332 (cf. commentary on no. 17). It is usually thought that this inscription records Alexander's orders issued after that recovery of Chios, reestablishing the democratic constitution under which Chios had supported him, restoring to Chios the democrats who had been exiled the previous year and arranging for the punishment of the oligarchs who had supported Memnon, imposing a garrison until the restored democracy settled down (the garrison was in fact withdrawn in 331), and exacting a contribution to Alexander's fleet. A.J. Heisserer has argued that Chios supported Philip's generals Attalus and Parmenio in 336, defected to the Persians in 335 and was recovered by Alexander in 334, and that it is after this recovery that Alexander's orders were given: our evidence for that period is so scanty that its silence is not fatal to the theory, and the reference to the fleet would make better sense in 334 than in 332. Another inscription (not in this collection) contains a second letter from Alexander to Chios, referring to the trials of men on a charge of "barbarism" (i.e. supporting the Persians) and granting a special amnesty to a man who was loyal to Alexander and had helped the enemy only under compulsion.

The prytanis Disitheus will have been the eponymous magistrate in whose term of office Alexander's letter was received (cf. the Introduction, p. vii, and nos. 17, 23). Twenty triremes was the same number as Alexander took from Athens. The paragraph beginning at 10 shows that the island states were incorporated in the League of Corinth (cf. no. 13 with commentary): in theory it will be by virtue of her membership of the league that Chios was required to contribute to Alexander's forces.

Alexander the Great and Priene, 331 (?)

(A: <u>Inschriften von Priene</u> 156, <u>SIG</u>[3] 277, Tod 184;
B: <u>Inschriften von Priene</u> 1, Tod 185)

A   KING ALEXANDER DEDICATED THE TEMPLE TO ATHENA <u>POLIAS</u>.

B1   ⟨EDICT⟩ OF KING ALEXANDER.

B2   Those of the residents at Naulochum who are ⟨citizens⟩ of Priene shall be independent and free, occupying all their own land and houses in the city and their territory ⟨in the country⟩; those who are not Prienians shall live in whatever villages they want. —, Myrs— and the territory of P— I regard as my own, and those who live in these villages shall pay tribute; but I exempt the city of Priene from the <u>syntaxis</u>, and the garrison at . . .

B16   (The stone breaks off. Fragments of what follows seem to be concerned with the institution of a law-court.)

Inscribed on the temple of Athena <u>Polias</u> at Priene: A is intact; B, even where a translation is given, is far from complete, and the text is less than certain.

    Priene, north of Miletus. was refounded in the fourth century, possibly but not certainly by Alexander: he could easily have visited the site in his progress through Asia Minor in 334 (cf. commentary on no. 17), and Tod and earlier editors ascribed the inscription to that year; but Professor E. Badian has argued that B is a revision of Alexander's original settlement with Priene, and should perhaps be dated as late as 331. The Greek cities of the Asiatic mainland, like those of the Aegean (cf. commentary on no. 18) were made members of the League of Corinth, and since Alexander no longer required further reinforcements the Asiatic members were made to pay a Contribution (<u>syntaxis</u> — the word was taken over from the Second Athenian League: cf. commentary on no. 1). On Badian's interpretation Priene was originally made to pay a <u>syntaxis,</u> probably substantial, and had a garrison stationed in the city; as Alexander advanced into Syria and Egypt it was involved in the trouble created behind Alexander's back by Memnon (cf. commentary on nos. 17 and 18); subsequently it was recovered by Alexander, and B represents the revised settlement. Also Alexander acquired the privilege of dedicating the temple of Athena — no doubt in exchange for a substantial contribution to the building costs. S.M. Sherwin - White points out that the text of B was not inscribed until the third century: possibly it is only an extract from Alexander's edict and need not belong to a revised settlement.

    Athena was worshipped under the cult title <u>Polias</u> as the guardian deity of the city (cf. no. 9, from Athens). Naulochum was the harbour of Priene, near the mouth of the Maeander. The distinction between the citizens of Priene and the non-citizens suggests that in the recent troubles the citizens had been loyal to Alexander but the non-citizens had not: in Alexander's dealings with the non-Greeks the domains of the Persian King became the possessions of the Macedonian King, and the tribute formerly payable to the Persian King was now payable to Alexander.

20

Cyrene supplies Corn to Greek States, 330—26

(SEG ix 2, Tod 196)

1	Priest Sosias son of Calliades.	
2	Those to whom the city supplied corn when there was a famine in Greece:—	
5	To Athens:	100,000 ⟨medimni⟩;
	* to Olympias:	60,000;
	to Argos:	50,000;
	to Larisa:	50,000;
	to Corinth:	50,000;
10	to Cleopatra:	50,000;
	to Rhodes:	30,000;
	to Sicyon:	30,000;
	* to Meliboea:	20,000;
	* to Megara:	20,000;
15	to Tenos (?):	20,000;
	to Lesbos (?):	15,000;
	to Thera:	15,000;
	* to the Oetaeans:	15,000;
	* to Ambracia:	15,000;
20	to Leucas:	15,000;
	to Carystus:	15,000;
22	+ to Olympias:	12,600;
24	to Atrax in Thessaly:	10,000;
25	to Cythnus:	10,000;
	to Opus:	10,000;
	to Cydonia:	10,000;
	to Cos:	10,000;
	to Paros:	10,000;
30	to Delphi:	10,000;
	* to Cnossus:	10,000;

	to Tanagra in Boeotia:	10,000;
	to Gortyn:	10,000;
	to Elis:	10,000;
35	to Palaerus in Acarnania:	10,000;
	+ to Megara:	10,000;
37	+ to Meliboea:	8,500;
39	to Phlius:	8,000;
40	to Hermione:	8,000;
41	+ to the Oetaeans:	6,400;
43	to Troezen:	6,000;
	to Plataea:	6,000;
45	to Iulis on Ceos:	5,000;
	* to Aegina:	5,000;
	to Astypalaea:	5,000;
	* to Cythera:	5,000;
	to Hyrtacina:	5,000;
50	+ to Aegina:	5,000;
	to Carthaea on Ceos:	4,000;
	+ to Cythera:	3,100;
	to Ceos:	3,000;
	to Illyria:	3,000;
55	to Coresus on Ceos:	3,000;
56	+ to Ambracia:	1,500;
58	to the Icetyrians (?):	1,000;
	+ to Cnossus:	900.

The text is almost complete, and there are no uncertainties apart from the names in lines 15, 16 and 58.

The inscription lists, in descending order of quantity, supplies of corn from Cyrene to the Greek states during the famine from which they suffered in the early 320's. The Greek verb used need not mean more than "supplied" — probably at the standard price or a slightly reduced price rather than free of charge. Eight recipients seem to have been sent two separate shipments: I have marked their first entry with an asterisk and their second with an obelus.

Cyrene (in North Africa, due south of the Greek mainland) was colonised from the island of Thera about 630 B.C.; the priest of Apollo (l. 1) was the eponymous magistrate (cf. the Introduction, p. vii). The measure used is probably the Aeginetan medimnus, equivalent to rather more than two bushels: the total amount of corn supplied is 805,000 medimni, or rather more than 1¾ million bushels. The recipients are distributed throughout mainland Greece, Crete and the Aegean islands: a notable omission is Sparta, which had refused to acknowledge the supremacy of Alexander the Great (cf. commentary on nos. 13, 21; Cyrene did so in 332/1, when Alexander was in Egypt); Olympias (ll. 6, 22) and Cleopatra (l. 10) are Alexander's mother and sister (cf. commentary on no. 10: after the death of Alexander of Epirus in 331, Olympias seized power there and Cleopatra fled to Macedon).

Athens honours Eudemus of Plataea, 329

(IG ii² 351 + 624, SIG³ 288, Tod 198)

1   OF EUDEMUS OF PLATAEA.

2   In the archonship of Aristophon ⟨330/29⟩; in the ninth prytany, of
    Leontis; when Antidorus son of Antinous, of Paeania, was secretary; on
    11 Thargelion (xi), on the nineteenth of the prytany; the question was
    put by Antiphanes (?) of Euonymum, ⟨chairman⟩ of the proedri; resolved
    by the people; Lycurgus son of Lycophron, of Butadae, proposed:—

11 Since Eudemus previously offered to make a contribution of 4,000
    drachmae to the people towards the war if it were necessary, and has
    now contributed 1,000 yoke ⟨of oxen⟩ for the building of the Stadium
    and the Panathenaic Theatre, and has sent all these before the Panathenaea
    as he promised; the people shall resolve:

21 To praise Eudemus son of Philurgus, of Plataea, and crown him with an
    olive crown for his goodwill towards the people of Athens; and he shall
    rank among the benefactors of the people of Athens, himself and his
    descendants, and shall have ⟨the right⟩ to acquire land and a house ⟨in
    Attica⟩ and to perform military service and to pay the eisphorae with
    the Athenians.

33 The secretary of the council shall record this decree and erect it on the
    acropolis; and for the inscription of the stele the treasurer of the people
    shall provide — drachmae from the people's fund for expenditure on decrees.

Some letters are missing, but the only uncertainties are the name of the chairman of the
proedri (I give the restoration of J. Pečírka, The Formula for the Grant of Enktesis in Attic
Inscriptions [1966], 69—70) and the amount of money to be spent on the stele. Comparison
with another inscription from the same month (not in this collection) shows that the date
has been wrongly given in the paragraph beginning at 2: 11 Thargelion (xi) 330/29 was not
the nineteenth but the twenty-ninth day of the prytany of Leontis.

The Greeks had to accept Alexander's succession to Philip, but they did so with
some reluctance. Many of them hoped that he would be defeated by the Persians, and some
maintained diplomatic contact with Persia. In 331 King Agis of Sparta (which had never
submitted to Macedon: cf. commentary on nos. 13, 20) took advantage of a disturbance in
Thrace to head a Greek revolt against Macedon; but Antipater, Alexander's deputy in

Macedon, quickly settled matters in Thrace and marched south with a large army to defeat and kill Agis outside Megalopolis, in the Peloponnese (probably still in 331; but some believe that the revolt ran from summer 331 to spring 330). The addition of Athens' sea power could have made the revolt far more serious, and some Athenians wanted to join in (though Demosthenes seems to have shown less than his usual zeal); but Demades, the Athenian politician most loyal to Macedon in Alexander's reign, persuaded the Athenians to keep out of trouble. This revolt may well be the war for which Eudemus had offered 4,000 drachmae "if it were necessary". Instead he contributed 1,000 yoke of oxen to help in the building either of the Panathenaic Stadium alone (in which case "Theatre" denotes the accommodation for the audience surrounding the Stadium proper) or of that and the Theatre of Dionysus (in which case the text of the decree contains a second error, and "Panathenaic" should be attached not to "Theatre" but to "Stadium" instead). The public buildings erected at this time are one aspect of a policy associated with the author of this decree, Lycurgus (on whom see also no. 16 with commentary), who for a period roughly coinciding with Alexander's reign exercised a general financial control in Athens (though the constitutional basis of his power is uncertain): the city's finances were put on a firmer footing, festivals were reorganised, public buildings were erected, the system of national service for young Athenians entering on their duties as citizens was revised, and the fleet was made larger than it had ever been before. The military aspect of Lycurgus' programme suggests that he wanted Athens to be ready to rise against Macedon when a suitable opportunity occurred; and his mention here of Eudemus' original offer (paragraph beginning at 11) may indicate that he was one of those who wanted Athens to join Agis' revolt.

Plataea, on the Boeotian side of the mountain range separating Attica from Boeotia, was for most of its history closely associated with Athens, and in conflict with the Boeotian federation led by Thebes. It had been destroyed by Thebes in 373/2 in the course of the expansion which embarrassed Athens (cf. commentary on no. 1), and was refounded after Philip's victory at Chaeronea in 338 (cf. commentary on no. 13). Eudemus is a citizen of Plataea, but the privileges voted to him suggest that he is resident in Athens as a metic (cf. no. 14, paragraph beginning at 22, with commentary).

22

Athens sends a Colony to the Adriatic, 325/4

(part of IG ii² 1629, SIG³ 305, Tod 200)

165   Decree in accordance with which Miltiades took over the triremes, quadriremes and triaconters, and the equipment:—

170   Cephisophon son of Lysiphon, of Cholargus, proposed:—

171   For the good fortune of the people of Athens; so that what the people have resolved concerning the colony to the Adriatic may be accomplished as quickly as possible, the people shall resolve:

178   The epimeletae of the dockyards shall hand over to the trierarchs their ships and equipment in accordance with the resolutions of the people, and the trierarchs who have been appointed shall bring them alongside the jetty in the month of Munychion (x) before the tenth and present them ready for sailing. The people shall crown the first to bring up his ship with a gold crown of 500 drachmae, the second ⟨with a crown⟩ of 300 drachmae, and the third ⟨with a crown⟩ of 200; and the herald of the council shall proclaim the crowns at the contest of the Thargelia. The apodectae shall allocate the money for the crowns, so that the trierarchs' eagerness to win the esteem of the people may be apparent.

204   So that the pleas ⟨of the trierarchs⟩ may be introduced ⟨into court⟩, the thesmothetae shall enlist courts of 201 for the general appointed to be in charge of the symmories, in the month of Munychion (x) on the second and the fifth, and the treasurers of the goddess ⟨Athena⟩ shall provide the salaries for the courts in accordance with the law.

217   So that the people shall have for all time their own commerce and corn transport; and so that, when their own naval base has been established, a watch may be kept against the Etruscans, and that the founder Miltiades and the settlers may be able to use their own fleet, and that the Greeks and barbarians sailing the sea and they themselves may be able to sail into the Athenian naval base, having their ships and everything else secure and knowing that . . .

(lacuna)

233   . . . If any one does not do each of the things he has been ordered, in accordance with this decree, whether he be an official or a private citizen, the man who fails ⟨in his duty⟩ shall owe 10,000 drachmae sacred to Athena, and the euthynus and his paredri shall be obliged to condemn him or they shall owe ⟨this sum⟩.

242   The council of five hundred shall take care of the dispatch, punishing the disorderly among the trierarchs in accordance with the laws. The prytany shall hold meetings of the council on the jetty continually until the dispatch is completed.

251   The people shall choose also as apostoleis ten men from all the Athenian ⟨citizens⟩, and those who are chosen shall take care of the dispatch as ordered by the council.

258   It shall be possible for the council and the prytany if they take care of
        the dispatch to be crowned by the people with a gold crown of 1,000
        drachmae.

264   If there is anything lacking in this decree about the dispatch, the council
        shall have power to vote ⟨the necessary provisions⟩, so long as it does
        not undo anything voted by the people.

270   All this shall be for the defence of the country.

This decree is included in a large document containing the inventory of the epimeletae
(curators) of the dockyards for 325/4 (the epimeletae were an annual board, generally
responsible for the dockyards and everything that they contained, who published a list of
ships, equipment, debts, &c., handed over from one board to the next): there are sizeable
restorations before the lacuna; after it the text is intact.

Literary sources for the period of Alexander's reign concentrate on him and on the
Greeks' dealings with him to the exclusion of almost all else; and Athens' colony in the
Adriatic is known only from this inscription. Attempts to safeguard the corn supply are
natural after the shortage of the early 320's (cf. commentary on no. 20), and there are other
signs that the Athenians were troubled by Etruscan pirates at this time. It is clear from the
paragraph beginning at 171 that what we have here is simply a supplementary decree, to
hasten the carrying out of what had already been decided in principle.

Miltiades, the founder of the colony, was a descendant of the Miltiades who defeated
the Persians at Marathon in 490. Triremes, ships with three banks of oars, had been the standard Greek warships since about the beginning of the fifth century; quadriremes and quinque-
remes, with two banks of oars and more than one man to an oar, were introduced from
Phoenicia in the second half of the fourth century; some still larger ships were built, but the
quinquereme became standard. Triaconters, with thirty oars in all, were smaller boats.
Trierarchs were rich citizens given the public duty (liturgy) of paying the running costs of a
warship for a year. In the fifth century one man was responsible for one ship, and usually
sailed with it; in the first half of the fourth century this became too great a burden to impose
on one man, and after a period in which shared trierarchies were the rule a law of Periander
(357) distributed the fleet's costs evenly over the 1,200 richest citizens, organised for admin-
istrative purposes in groups called symmories. In 340 Demosthenes restricted liability to the
300 richest citizens, now contributing in proportion to their wealth; and there may have been
further changes later: this decree seems to point to a return to the old practice, by which a
trierarch was personally responsible for his ship.

The Thargelia was a festival of Apollo celebrated on 6 and 7 Thargelion (xi). For the
apodectae and their allocation (merismos: the cognate verb is used here) of public money,
see the Introduction, p.vii. The pleas referred to in the paragraph beginning at 204 are claims
for exemption from the trierarchy: they are to be decided by jury courts, presided over by
the general in charge of the symmories (for the board of generals and the introduction of
regular jobs for individual generals cf. commentary on no. 3), the executive officer responsible
for the operation of the trierarchic system. The thesmothetae (six in number: with the archon,
the basileus and the polemarch they formed the college of nine archons) supervised the complicated procedure by which juries were empanelled and allocated to the different courts

(and themselves presided over some of the courts); the treasury of Athena was apparently the financial authority through which in the fourth century payment to jurors was made (there is no other evidence). There were ten euthyni, each with two paredri, or assistants, to whom complaints might be made against officials on their retirement: these could dismiss the charge or refer it to the appropriate jury court. Apostoleis (dispatchers) were an extra-ordinary appointment.

There are other fourth-century decrees in which the council is authorised to pass supplementary resolutions to fill any gaps which are discovered in the original decree: cf. no. 7, paragraph beginning at 34, and, from Mytilene, no. 23, paragraph beginning at 37. To label a decree "for the defence of the country" was apparently to place it in a specially privileged category; but it is not known what privileges this conferred on the decree.

23

Restoration of Exiles to Mytilene, 330's or 324

(IG XII.ii 6, OGIS 2, Tod 201)

1   . . . The basileis shall favour the returned ⟨exile⟩ on the grounds that the
     one who remained in the city has been guilty of fraud. But if any of the
     returned does not abide by this settlement, he shall not receive any
     property from the city, nor enter into possession of any of the property
     which those who remained in the city have ceded to him; but those who
     ceded it to him, of those who remained in the city, shall enter into
     possession of this, and the generals shall transfer the property back to
     the man who remained in the city, on the grounds that the man who
     returned has not been reconciled; and the basileis shall favour the man
     who remained in the city on the grounds that the one who returned has
     been guilty of fraud, and if any one brings a lawsuit concerning these
     matters it shall not be brought into court by the peridromi or the diascopi
     or any other official.

13   The generals, the basileis, the peridromi and the diascopi shall take care,
     if everything is not done as is written in this decree, that they condemn
     the man who fails to do any of the things written in this decree, so that
     there may be no dispute between those who have returned and those who
     remained in the city, but all those who have been reconciled may live
     without suspecting one another and without plotting against one another
     and may abide by the reply of the king and the settlement in this decree.

21   The people shall choose twenty men as mediators, ten from those who
     have returned and ten from those who remained in the city: they shall
     watch earnestly and take care that there is no dispute between those who

have returned and those who have remained in the city. They shall act over disputed property most of all so that those who have returned may be reconciled with those in the city and with one another; or, failing that, that they may be as just as possible, and may all abide by the settlement pronounced by the king, and by the agreement, and may live in the city and the country in agreement with another.

30 Concerning money, after the reconciliation has been accepted as far as possible, and concerning the oath which the citizens are to swear, concerning all these things the men who are chosen shall report to the people what they have agreed among themselves, and the people shall listen to them and deliberate as they think advantageous. And if the people think that what they have agreed among themselves is advantageous, they shall vote also for those returning in the prytany of Smithinas what they have voted for the others.

37 If anything is missing from this decree, the council shall have the right of decision in these matters. When the decree has been ratified by the people, the whole people on the twentieth of the month, after the sacrifice, shall pray to the gods that the reconciliation between those who have returned and those who remained in the city may be for the safety and happiness of all the citizens: all the public priests and priestesses shall open the temples, and the people shall come to pray. The sacrifices which the people vowed when they sent the messengers to the king shall be offered annually on the king's birthday: there shall be present at the sacrifice the twenty men and the messengers sent to the king from those who remained in the city and from those who have returned.

49 The treasurers shall record this decree . . .

A quarter to a half of each line has been restored: some of the details are uncertain, but the general sense is reliable enough.

On returning to central Persia from the east, in 324, Alexander punished a number of provincial governors, and issued a general order to all governors to disband their mercenary armies. This, together with demobilisations from his own army, produced a flow of mercenaries to Greece, many of whom assembled at Taenarum, in the Peloponnese. It was perhaps in order to break up this growing army, waiting for employment, that Alexander ordered that all Greek exiles (with a few exceptions), a class which provided many of the mercenaries of the fourth century, were to be restored to their cities. Athens and Aetolia objected: other cities accepted the order, but a good deal of difficulty arose over the property which had once belonged to the exiles. Most editors have taken this text to be part of a decree putting that order from Alexander into effect in Mytilene, on the island of Lesbos; but some have thought that the upheavals of the 330's, at the beginning of Alexander's war against Persia, provide a better context (cf. commentary on nos. 17, 18). The case for the earlier dating has been strengthened by the discovery of another decree of Mytilene, attempting to secure concord among the citizens after a restoration of democracy: that most probably belongs to the 330's, and the two inscriptions should belong to the same context. In either case, the decree translated here supplements an earlier enactment: messengers have been sent to Alexander from both parties, presumably to consult him on details (paragraph beginning at 37), and he has replied (paragraph beginning at 13); some exiles have not yet returned, but are presumably waiting to see how the reconciliation works (reference to those returning in the prytany of Smithinas, in the paragraph beginning at 30).

The inscription reveals an abundance of public authorities in Mytilene. There is a sovereign assembly, and a council which can be authorised to fill any gaps discovered in the assembly's decree (as in Athens: no. 7, paragraph beginning at 34, and no. 22, paragraph beginning at 264). There is an eponymous magistrate with the title prytanis cf. the Introduction, p. vii, and nos. 17, 18). There are generals, basileis, peridromi and diascopi, who are all involved in enforcing the settlement. The twenty mediators are, of course, an extraordinary appointment.

CONCORDANCE

IG	SIG[3]	OGIS	Tod	This collection
ii[2] 43	147	—	123	1
ii[2] 123	192	—	156	6
ii[2] 124	190	—	153	3
ii[2] 125	191	—	154	4
ii[2] 126	—	—	151	2
ii[2] 127	196	—	157	7
ii[2] 212	206	—	167	9
ii[2] 226	228	—	173	10
ii[2] 228	255	—	174	11
ii[2] 233	256	—	175	12
ii[2] 236	260	—	177	13
ii[2] 237	259	—	178	14
ii[2] 337	280	—	189	16
ii[2] 351 + 624	288	—	198	21
ii[2] 1629	305	—	200	22
vii 2418	201	—	160	8
XII.ii 6	—	2	201	23
XII.ii 526	—	8	191	17
XII.vii 5	193	—	152	5
—	283	—	192	18
Inschriften von Priene 1			185	19 (B)
Inschriften von Priene 156	SIG[3] 277		184	19 (A)
SEG ix 2			196	20
Hesp. xxi 1952, pp. 355–9, no. 5	SEG xii 87		—	15

970S31B

£ 3.50

PRINTED BY: STAMFORD HILL STATIONERS.   TEL: 01–802 5222